LOVE TEACHING

M. Ming

We love
because he
first loved us.
1 John 4:19

LOVE
TEACHING

Cover Art: Sally Ginnow

Thank you, Sally.

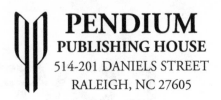

PENDIUM
PUBLISHING HOUSE
514-201 DANIELS STREET
RALEIGH, NC 27605

For information, please visit our Web site at
www.pendiumpublishing.com

PENDIUM Publishing and its logo
are registered trademarks.

Love Teaching
by M. Ming

ISBN: 978-1-944348-62-5

PUBLISHER'S NOTE

This book is printed on acid-free paper.

CONTENTS

ACKNOWLEDGEMENTS

When life has been challenging, I have often wondered, "Why me, Lord?" In my discouragement, I have tried to rally by asking the Lord to use my difficulties, pains, and hurts for His glory so that the pain suffered would not be in vain. While praying those types of prayers, the Lord has brought to mind different passages of Scripture to calm my spirit. One of the recurring Scriptures that came to mind, 2 Corinthians 1:3-4 (New International Version), has been most impactful for many reasons.

> *Praise be to the God and Father of our Lord Jesus Christ, the Father of compassion and the God of all comfort, who comforts us in all of our troubles, so that we can comfort those in any trouble with the comfort we ourselves receive from God. For just as we share abundantly in the sufferings of Christ, so also our comfort abounds through Christ.*

It is because of His abundant compassion that this book has been written. I MUST express my gratitude to and love for the Author and Perfecter of my faith, my Lord and Savior

Jesus Christ, who inspired and called me to His service in the field of education as an educator and has moved me to share what I have learned from Him while in His service.

My husband, Fuller Ming, Jr., is a continual faith-filled influence and loving companion in my life. Praise be to God for my husband, His gift to me. My husband's unwavering encouragement and commitment continue to push me forward when I want to procrastinate or when negative thoughts threaten to stop me from forging ahead.

My mother, stepmother, daughter, and son – whom I love deeply and am honored to have in my life; I am grateful for them and their love for me.

My life coach – my confidante, cheerleader, friend, and counselor for more than five years: She has given me godly counsel; encouraged me in my faith; and inspired me to pursue Him and His calling, which includes writing this book. She is one of God's precious gifts to me. I love her and am grateful to the Lord for her support and guidance.

Lastly, I thank my editor, who has been able to take my words and find the meaning from them, rephrase them, and bring out the depth of my thoughts. I have needed you, and you have been there for me. Thank you.

> Now to him who is able to do immeasurably more than all we ask or imagine, according to his power that is at work within us, to him be glory in the church and in Christ Jesus throughout all generations, for ever and ever! Amen. (Eph. 3:20-21 New International Version)

My passion is that students exercise their God-given gifts of heart and mind to His glory.

We Love Because
He First Loved Us.

This is how God showed his love among us: He sent his one and only Son into the world that we might live through him. (1 Jn. 4:9)

We love because he first loved us.
(1 Jn. 4:19)

Love is Kind

...love is kind. (1 Cor. 13:4b)

CHAPTER 1

SORROW

Be merciful to me, Lord, for I am in distress;
my eyes grow weak with sorrow,
my soul and body with grief.
(Ps. 31:9)

I was a young 23-year-old teacher eager to show minority high schoolers that they could succeed with hard work, grit, and determination. I pushed my students to move beyond their perceived limitations. My good intentions broadly encompassed my students as a whole, but my true purpose as an educator who is also a Christian became personal in one tragic moment.

A student of mine had begun to carve his name, Shaka, into the wooden desk where he sat. He never brought the textbook he'd been given into our Geometry class, and he arrived without pencils, paper, or any other necessities. Observing these behaviors, I concluded that he was not trying to work hard in MY class. In my mind, this was most definitely about ME. I found his behavior irritating and annoying, to say the least.

I'd met this student, Shaka Franklin, the year before when he was a tenth-grade varsity football player. He was a gifted athlete with a smile that warmed the entire hallway and any room he entered. He would wave at the teachers and greet us with pleasantries that I looked forward to daily, so when I saw his name on my Geometry roster as an eleventh-grader, I thought it would be fun to have him in my class. I was looking forward to teaching such an enthusiastic child.

The year before had been my first as a full-time high school teacher, and I'd experienced classes that were difficult to teach due to rude students or parents, unkind administrators, or similar circumstances. I thought I could count on having this one student each day who would be kind and pleasant. I was looking for a 'do-over' year where I could start afresh. I would set a pleasant tone, pray more for my students, and serve God honorably in this secular public-school.

Come, let us bow down in worship, let us kneel before the Lord our Maker; for he is our God and we are the people of his pasture, the flock under his care. (Ps. 95:6-7)

However, Shaka did not smile or greet his teachers as he had the year before. He took a seat in the back despite my request that he sit in the front row. When I gave books out, he took one but never brought it to class after that. Only when I provided paper and pencil would he do the classwork assignment. I queried his tenth-grade teachers about this negligent behavior, but they had no insights to offer me. After a few assignments were submitted, his grade was a D, which seemed quite out of character for him. I began to wonder if my original perceptions of him were incorrect and if I had misjudged the contribution that he could make to the Geometry class. I called his father to express my concerns about his behavior and grades, hoping he might encourage Shaka to perk up and become the student I'd expected. Instead, after my conversation with his dad, he arrived in class the next day more determined to do nothing for ME because I had called his father.

Shrugging this off as an adolescent meltdown, I dismissed his anger and slight temper tantrum and decided that he wasn't the student I'd known from the previous year after all. I dishonored him in my heart and cast away the concerns I had, taking his behaviors personally and holding on to my perceptions as if they defined him. I mean, a summer can change a person, especially a teen whose hormones were raging. Besides, I needed to focus on teaching as best I could, or so I thought. On a side note, Geometry was not my best subject in high school, so teaching it required lots of preparation, leaving me rather tense about the class as a whole.

As time went on and parent-teacher conference night loomed, Shaka became less angry but more sad, sullen, and withdrawn. The varsity football star no longer etched his name in the desk or slouched in defiance but lay sorrowfully with his head to the side. Alarmed, I spoke with his father, Les Franklin, convincing him that he needed to act quickly to address whatever was causing his son such dejection, not to mention poor grades. I was beginning to care about Shaka, and not just the impact he was having on my self-importance as his Geometry teacher.

His father promised to speak with Shaka after work the next day, which was a Friday and also a game day. As customary, the football players wore dress clothes, and Shaka wore a suit to school. With his sharp attire and improved countenance, he seemed like the teenager I had been missing all semester. That evening, Les came home from work planning to speak with his son about his demeanor, only to find him dead from a well-planned suicide[1].[2] Shaka had put a revolver to his head. He hadn't left a note, but we in the school community would learn later that the Franklin family had been facing challenging illnesses. We realized that we had missed a sign of suicide preparation – the dispersal of personal belongings to others. Shaka had been giving his precious possessions to his friends throughout the previous summer. Unfortunately, these friends didn't know each other well enough to collude regarding the gifts they received. It was as though a piece of the puzzle was missing for each of us.

Maybe the illnesses in his family were the source of his grief. Those of us who mourned him tried to make sense of how a handsome 16-year-old with such promise, bestowed with gifts of intellect, athleticism, attractiveness, and health, would take his own life.

For many years, it haunted me that my focus had been on the impact Shaka's behaviors were having on MY classroom, MY ability to teach Geometry, and MY peace as an educator. I have learned many lessons as a teacher, but the most poignant have come from Shaka.

---

[1]   See information in Appendix A for Suicide Prevention information

[2]   The Shaka Franklin Foundation was created after Shaka's suicide. See Appendix A for more information on Shaka

CHAPTER 2

SINCERITY

Love must be sincere. Hate what is evil;
cling to what is good.
(Rom. 12:9)

"Do something good. Feel something real." This was a slogan for the Points of Light Foundation, which was founded by former President George H.W. Bush. The slogan and motto quickly became a pithy saying in the 1990s, its espousers believing that by doing something good, you could find value and worth as a person.

The truth is, to care for others authentically, your goal has to be their interests above your own, not feeling something real for yourself. Authentic kindness lies in true humility, which requires genuine sacrifice. Selfish ambition and vanity can fuel giving, but only to a point. To sincerely value another above yourself, you must be secure in knowing Whose you are. When you are anchored in Christ's love and encouraged by the Lord, there is no reason to seek merit by providing charity to others. Instead, the grace you show is overflow from your own grateful, encouraged, and beloved heart toward another soul in need of care. This is God's loving-kindness flowing through you.

As a Christian educator, your fuel must be your relationship with the Lord. Be thankful every day for your life and the beauty around you. Drink in His love and forgiveness. If we do not keep Him as our focus, we will seek acceptance and love elsewhere. The kindness we extol is fleeting when our focus is on others' assessment of us rather than the Lord's.

Educators might seek this type of affirmation in the classroom from their students out of the sense of "doing something good" and expecting to "feel something real." However, young people from Pre-K through 12th grade need encouragement, guidance, and continual compassion as you seek their best interests. They are unable and ill-equipped to provide you, their educator, with the appreciation that you may crave. Of course, some joys will come from teaching these students who are precious gifts from the Lord. Please understand my point; I am not saying you won't have fulfilling experiences as a teacher. There will come satisfaction in those 'Aha!' moments when your students finally understand a concept you have labored to teach them. But you can't just wait for those moments to realize the crucial role we play as role models and God-given ambassadors of His love. We represent the Lord to them! Our citizenship is in heaven, and we are here to address His concerns in the lives of others. Our love must be sincere.

For God so loved the world that he gave his one and only Son, that whoever believes in him shall not perish but have eternal life. (Jn. 3:16)

CHAPTER 3

TIMES OF TROUBLE

The Lord is a refuge for the oppressed, a stronghold
in times of trouble.
(Ps. 9:9)

At six years old, I would haul my Dr. Seuss books to the neighbor's apartment patio to instruct her – and any dolls we had – on the lessons I had learned that week in school. My biggest issue then was that although the neighbor girl benefited from the lessons, she neither helped me carry the books to her apartment or back to mine. At any rate, I think that teaching was my calling from an early age. I was in 7th grade when I decided I wanted to teach math. My love for education – both learning and teaching others – continues to this day.

My journey toward becoming a teacher might have started when I was young, but I was not born into it. Education was not on the mind of my ancestors. Painful experiences in my life revealed God's love for me and transformed me into a teacher with a heart for Him. The story I will share illustrates how adversity drew me to Jesus.

To help you understand why I was drawn to teaching and ministering to teenagers, I will start at the beginning – over twenty years ago, with my own troubling times as a young person.

My mother's grandmother (Nana) was born into slavery on a plantation in North Carolina. After many trials (including domestic violence, which resulted in a near-death experience for her when she was thrown down a flight of stairs – for the second time), she fled to D.C., leaving her children behind. Her escape saved her life and set off a chain of events leading to my future success.

How does slavery fit into all of this? Where is teaching in all of this? The picture of all enslaved persons singing Negro spirituals and believing in God did not include my family of origin. My mom's family's lostness began with those who were willing to sell and buy people, *despite claiming to follow Christ,* and continued when my family, consciously or not, decided not to follow Christ at all. Godlessness takes a toll on people and families; this is one lesson I learned first-hand. The toll is pain, suffering, and sorrow resulting from the 'passive wrath of God.' Our family reaped the consequences of not following the Lord, but though we suffered, there was a light that shone in the darkness.

Here is where God came into my mom's story, and therefore, my own. My mother's parents were deployed overseas with the Army, so she was living with her grandparents for a period of time. There was a neighbor on Nana's street who offered to take Mom to church when she was a child. Mom sang in the children's choir and learned of the goodness of God. She accepted that God was real.

When life at home with her grandmother became difficult due to continued domestic violence against her, she felt that she needed to leave the house before she resorted to violence as well. She was able to move back in with her parents, although she experienced continued challenges until she met and married my father.

Her marriage to my father lasted five years, enduring the miscarriage of my brother, Michael, and then my own complicated birth due to umbilical cord entanglement and breech positioning. However, when I was a year old, my mom arrived home to find a note from my father saying that he was leaving her. He removed his belongings from their home prior to her arrival home from work. As a result of his leaving, she thought God had abandoned her. When someone takes off that way, they don't just leave the spouse but also the children. I, too, felt abandoned, broken, and defective as a person.

My dad became someone I saw in the summers when I was in elementary school, but he traveled frequently, so I spent more time with my kind and generous stepmom during my summer visits. I lived with my mother during the elementary school years, but ultimately, I longed for a nuclear family unit: my mom and my dad, 24/7 and 365 days of the year, happily married to each other. But as it was, I traveled every summer to another state where Dad lived. When I was in first grade, that travel was on a train because he didn't live too far from D.C., but when I was seven, he moved out West, and I had to travel alone on a five-hour flight. From then until I was twenty years old, flying between homes twice a year became my life.

Through all of this, my mom learned common sense and human love that her grandmother emphasized, and Godly love from going to worship with the neighbor friend. Both of these seeds of love were passed on to my children and me. God's love was extended to her through her neighbor, the children's choir, and her exposure to other believers. The Word of God was planted in her young life and the pain of her adulthood returned her to Him who gives life. Her education in God's word eventually became the foundation for major changes as an adult.

Mom's parents (my grandparents) paid for my private Christian elementary school education and even my hot lunch, for which I am now very grateful. At our school, we had a worship service weekly (sometimes daily), but I never attended worship outside of that. Mom felt at that time that God had abandoned her, so going to worship in a church was out of the question. She eventually remarried, but after a while, that became a difficult situation for both of us.

My stepdad had other children. One of his sons was my age and would come to visit our apartment regularly. Even though we were both in lower elementary school, he made inappropriate and impure gestures constantly when we were alone together. I hated when he came over, but I was not able to verbalize those issues until adulthood. My mom and stepfather argued frequently, and the continued unrest eventually led to our unexpected departure from the apartment one night and Mom and I getting our own apartment.

Food scarcity is the term now, but back when I was nine and ten years old, I would just say that I stayed hungry. We had moved quite far from my elementary school, so in order to get to school every day, Mom would put me on the metro alone. I would travel through the part of D.C. that passed St. Elizabeth's hospital and stop right across from it in front of a liquor store where drunk people would try to get onto the bus. I was scared every day of the way those people acted, so I would hold on tight to the pole right behind the bus driver. (Unfortunately, I had to transfer once. Miserable.) I carried a great deal of anxiety about this whole endeavor, but I loved my mom, so I was brave for her sake. In the meantime, Mom had challenges coping with issues from her past that led to difficulty in the present and resulted in a lack of funds for food. The hot lunch assistance from my grandparents allowed me to eat at school, which was a daily blessing. They lived in New Jersey, not near us, so I didn't realize then how much they were supporting me, but I am grateful to them both.

Due to the lack of funds, we had Campbell's Chicken with Stars soup so often that as a grown woman and a mom, when my own son asked for that soup because of the cool shapes, I became nauseated when I opened the can. The soup was fine, but the smell reminded me of those years. At age nine, when my stepmom picked me up from the airport for the summer, she was alarmed at my weight loss.

At the time, we had a gallon of water from the faucet in the refrigerator and cans of soup; there was no fruit or vegetable in sight for many months. I blocked out those memories until circumstances brought them back. For the food issues, it was my son's interest in Chicken with Stars. For my bus trip, it was a different experience.

I had taken a job in a different school in D.C. at the age of forty-six. During new hire teacher orientation, they piled all of the new hires into a tour bus to ride through the city. Their goal was to humanize the students we were going to teach by showing us their neighborhoods. The charter school system had established its elementary and middle schools where they could develop a sense of community.

11

It so happened that one of the schools was across the street from St. Elizabeth's Hospital. The liquor store with the bus stop was still there, and as our tour bus rolled into the parking lot of the school behind the liquor store, I began to weep unexpectedly and uncontrollably. Even after I got myself under control, I remained badly shaken as they walked us through the new school building. It took hours for me to process the cause of all of the pain.

I realized that I had blocked the childhood bus trips from my mind until that memory was awakened by seeing that area again. The fact that we happened to be on a bus as well helped the memory surface, I am certain.

While in elementary school, I had no one to speak to about any of this because neither my elementary school teachers nor any other of the school employees were approachable to me. I had no adult in my life to go to for comfort, solace, or refuge at that time. I felt utterly alone and unable to focus well in school during those times.

Because I was a sensitive child experiencing daily trauma, however seemingly insignificant, I was unable to learn as well as should have been possible for me. I was in survival mode; thriving was out of the question, especially without an outlet. A coach or supportive adult would have been a great blessing, but I was barely hanging on, with no respite even at school.

Remember, you can offer your students the gift of the Lord's refuge. In the name of God, you can be that refuge in times of trouble for them. Point them to the Lord so that they may learn to find refuge in Him.

CHAPTER 4

REJECTION

Restore us to yourself, Lord, that we may return;
renew our days as of old unless you have utterly
rejected us and are angry with us beyond measure.
(Lam. 5:21-22)

Due to the traumatic circumstances and financial difficulties that my mom and grandparents encountered during my sixth-grade year, Mom arranged for me to move out West with my father and stepmom to finish my middle and high school years in their excellent public-school district. Although this was an advantageous opportunity, in hindsight, I felt abandoned by life again and neglected in different ways by both parents and ultimately by God, whom I had learned about in my faith-based elementary school.

My father and stepmother had great jobs and earned a good, middle-class income. My stepmother managed money well, so when the opportunity to go to Europe with my choir arose, they were able to make a way. Over the years, we visited Hawaii and Mexico, and I learned to snow ski and ice fish. Dad provided a car for me, teaching me how to change the oil, add coolant, change a tire, and even replace the radiator when mine had a hole. I was given amazing experiences and opportunities because of living with them. However, all that glitters ain't gold, as they say.

In my new school, I was the only African-American student in any of my classes, although there were seven others in my graduating class of 485. Still, I was the only one not raised out West, which made me an outcast for another reason. It is an understatement to say that it was hard for me to fit in.

I was a quiet and reserved child and very uncomfortable in my new situation. Coming from inner-city D.C., this environment felt unwelcoming, and I resolved to interact as seldom as possible with others. However, a quiet and reserved White female student did reach out to me, and we became friends. One day while we were hanging out together at school, we decided we should have a sleepover at her house. She called her mom to ask if I could come home with her, and I noticed that her expression changed when her mom asked a question. "Why do you want to know what color skin she has? She's Black. Why does that matter?"

Her mother's voice was loud enough for me to hear, and my friend's face paled. She hung up and told me that she was forbidden to speak to me, sit near me in class, or eat lunch with me ever again. Crushing. She obeyed her mom from that moment on, to the letter of the law.

I retreated further into myself, trying to determine how to proceed from there. What if I made another White friend, and this happened again? I did not think I could stomach that, so I vowed to keep my distance from everyone for the rest of middle school. Still, at different points in time, my courage rose, and I joined the orchestra, choir, and drama club. Part of me wanted to persevere and meet people despite my fear.

In my senior year of high school, I had a boyfriend who was White. After about a month of dating, we visited his home so I could meet his mom. She welcomed me, and I enjoyed being at their house from time to time. Eventually, it seemed that he had become uninterested in talking to me at school or on the phone. I didn't understand what had changed. It was many years later, while I was in my thirties, that I learned he had been told to break up with me. He didn't know how to do it and didn't really want to, so he handled it by becoming more and more distant. We caught up with each other on Facebook, and I found out that his mother had forbidden him to date me because I'm Black. Hurtful. When rejection is due to something that can't be changed, the helplessness and hopelessness can be suffocating, seeming to choke the life out of you.

At seventeen, my life felt so complicated that I didn't want to live anymore, and I developed suicidal thoughts and ideation with a concrete plan. My boyfriend's rejection, other assaults that year, and my father's depression and drinking causing verbal negativity – all while feeling suffocated for being Black culminated in absolute misery with my very existence. I wished to end my life during my senior year of high school and struggled with the same thoughts again in my freshman year of college.

I called my former boyfriend, hoping that maybe he would care. I told him that I was going to take all of my dad's blood pressure medication to kill myself. He tried to talk me out of it, and the way I hung up caused him to call the police to tell them to check on me.

When they arrived, the police were condescending and rude, as well as abrupt. Because I was a minor, I had to be placed in the home of a relative, according to them. They called my father's brother and his wife to come and get me. The police stayed until my aunt arrived, and she called my father and stepmom, who were on a trip. They were exasperated that they had to come home early and that I couldn't stay home alone without creating drama. In addition, my father took the keys to my car in case I had plans to drive off a cliff.

My stepmother arranged for therapy sessions for our family, but dad struggled with being there and refused to address the counselor. His body language indicated shame, guilt, anger, defeat, and a host of other feelings. He kept his back to us the entire time, and neither he nor my stepmom came to any subsequent sessions. The counselor said that he couldn't help me much without my whole family present, so I stopped going.

Throughout all of this, I tried to behave and remain emotionally stable in my classes. I continued to feel a lack of belonging and rejected for being Black, so despite everything going on in my personal life, many of my teachers still did not *see* me, so they couldn't *see* my pain.

> Trust in him at all times, you people; pour out your
> hearts to him, for God is our refuge.
> (Ps. 62:8)

One night while waiting in a piano room in the theatre hallway for my audition time for the upcoming Spring musical, another classmate was in another piano room until his turn. He was someone I bantered with during the school day, so when he came to the door of the room I was practicing in, I opened it, thinking he just wanted to talk. I admit that I'd felt attracted to him, but our previous interactions never gave that away.

Instead of talking, he grabbed me and threw me to the floor, holding me down with his kneecaps on mine and one of his elbows on my arm. He began to unbutton my shirt with his free hand. I was pinned to the ground and had no idea what to do, so I just started to cry. I was seventeen. He was a Lacrosse player, and with his physicality, I felt trapped under a tank.

When I began to tear up, he abruptly got off of me and ran away. Later, he denied it had happened but admitted that he'd been eating hallucinogenic 'shrooms' and taking other drugs in tandem, so it was possible. He said that he was sorry if he had done what I said. I didn't tell anyone who could have taken any action. I told myself that I didn't want anyone to make a fuss over me, but the truth was I was afraid of being laughed at, blamed, vilified, or ignored.

Thus, I thought, "Fade into the background; be invisible as best you can. You live in a White world at this school. It is best to avoid standing out any more than you already do. Blend in!" The façade held, and no one knew that anything of consequence had occurred in my life.

In my attempt to blend in with the "White culture" I was immersed in at school and work, I went to a party that a co-worker from my job at McDonald's threw. I was still seventeen, and this was about four months after the incident at school. I went with a friend from school, and that night I tried my first shot of liquor. It only took one shot for me to become inebriated. My only other experience with alcohol had been my stepfather giving me a beer when I was nine and telling me that it was soda. I said it was the worst tasting soda I'd ever had, and all the adults had a great laugh at my expense.

With my inexperience, this shot of liquor was shocking to my system, and I quickly became woozy. The room seemed hazy, and the music suddenly sounded wonderful. I started dancing with this guy who had just come from using a marijuana-filled bong upstairs. He'd also been drinking. I had to sit – the wooziness and haziness were getting worse.

When the fog in my head cleared, I realized that he had raped me right there at the party. I had been utterly unable to stop it, resist it, or take control of my mind or body to free myself.

The owner of the home who threw the party was disgusted that I would 'allow' someone to do that to me. Unfortunately, he was also one of the shift managers at the McDonald's where I worked and continued to remind me of what a whore I was when we worked together. What he didn't know was that until that night, I had been a virgin.

The Lord works righteousness and justice for all the oppressed. (Ps. 103:6)

That experience, along with my stepbrother's inappropriate behaviors and the situation with the Lacrosse player in school, still affects me to this day. Albeit, those are to a much lesser degree, as retelling this particular story still causes me distress. Since my virginity was now ruined (in my mind), I felt demoralized and considered that even if there was a God, He no longer wanted me. I was damaged goods. We were all living for ourselves, with no righteous influence. Our actions reflected an ungodly perspective. God's loving response to the brokenness of my heart would have been as water to a thirsty soul, but I did not yet realize that it was Him I was missing.

I arrived home at about one in the morning, smelling of alcohol and weed. Driving under the influence is a bad idea, as most of us would agree, but I had to get away from that house. Even though the 30-mph limit felt like warp speed, I forced myself to drive at 31, knowing that if I drove too slowly, I'd be just as likely to attract the attention of the police – the last thing I wanted. To me, it added a little realness to the 'avoid being seen' tactic.

I had to tiptoe in and get to my room quickly to shut the door before breaking down in tears of self-loathing. I shouldn't have gone. And I'd left my friend there, passed out on their couch. What were they going to do to her?

Why did I drink anything? How stupid I was! I should have pushed him off of me. I should have screamed, but the alcohol had so affected my reflexes that all I'd been able to do was mutter for him to stop. I kept thinking, why didn't I do more? I cried and cried until my eyes hurt so badly that I thought they would fall out of my head in protest.

Again, I told no one. Why? I was ruined, unlovable, and damaged goods. Who would want to know, and more importantly, who would care?

Not long after this incident, Dad and my stepmom went away for a weekend alone, so I decided to have someone over to the house. One of the other eight black students from school was a young man I thought was cute. Maybe he would find me lovable. Again, I was searching for love in all the wrong places.

I asked him over. I created what I thought was a romantic atmosphere with the fireplace going and food out. Romance was not on his mind at all. The conversation went nowhere; he made a few phone calls and then left unceremoniously. I probably creeped him out, given that we barely knew each other, and the mood I tried to create was out of place.

I thought that I needed someone to believe in me and love me romantically to validate my worth, but what I really needed was to believe in Him and accept His love for me.

How priceless is your unfailing love, O God! People take refuge in the shadow of your wings. (Ps. 36:7)

About fifteen years ago, I found out that my psychology teacher's email address at the high school was still valid when he responded to an email I sent. I wrote to thank him for taking the time to talk to me about my dreams while I was in high school. I admit that in high school, I had a crush on him. He looked like John Denver, and I thought he was beautiful, so I hung around his office, hoping that we could talk.

He was one of the few teachers in my high school that I felt 'saw' me as a teenager he could encourage, not just his only Black student. He replied to my email that he was retiring soon and that he had no idea all of the negative things I'd outlined in the email had happened to me during high school. He remembered me as bubbly. It had seemed difficult to hide how much trouble I had in high school, but I'd apparently succeeded.

I had not chosen to live for God or acknowledge His ways but rather was trying to figure out how to live without Him. I gave up on decency and decided that none of it mattered anymore. Dying and wild living were just two sides of the same coin. Either one would destroy me.

So many of our students present fake smiles that hide battered lives. Being open to that possibility is our gift to the student who would rather be invisible than risk the rejection that comes with visibility. Be mindful that simply asking about their day, listening, and being present is encouraging them to believe they are valuable and priceless to the Lord.

As adults, we have our own drama and heartache, so being present for students sounds like a burdensome task, and to be sure, it sometimes is. However, your self-care is pursuing God, in whom you will find your strength, your worth, your calling, and your perspective as a teacher, which can elevate a student's perspective of their own life.

CHAPTER 5

HONOR

Do nothing out of selfish ambition or vain conceit.
Rather, in humility value others above yourselves,
not looking to your own interests but each of you to
the interests of the others. (Php. 2:3-4)

I am a trained soprano soloist. I began lessons at the age of fifteen, but my dad refused to pay for them. He wanted me to follow in his footsteps and take bass lessons instead. He was an extremely talented bassist in a jazz band and also played all the brass instruments in the Army band for the three years he was in the service.

I wanted to sing so badly I got a job at McDonald's to pay for my own lessons. I hoped to become a voice actress and studied acting on and off throughout my life. I really thought that I would make a terrific actress, singer, and musical theater performer. I didn't understand the hustle that goes into being an actor, but I was enamored by live theater, especially musical theater.

My high school theater program was well-known in our area. Our productions attracted so many that the brand-new theater was standing room only on every opening night during my four-year high school career. I loved the sound of the crowds and the smell of greasepaint. As the makeup crew chief, I learned techniques to make a fifteen-year-old look twice that age. I played in the pit orchestra as a bassist (admittedly not nearly as good as my father) and directed our senior musical 'Guys and Dolls,' and both were high points for me during those years.

However, dedicated as I was during my forays as costume crew chief, props manager, stage director, and student director, my day to act in the spotlight didn't come. I was never cast to act in any play.

I thought that I must be a lousy actress, which dashed my dreams. I stayed involved in the theater after high school by working at the Jewish Community Center during their production of 'My Fair Lady' as a props manager, but I really longed to be *on* the stage rather than behind it. My personality tells me that if something is true in the moment, it will always be so, and I have a difficult time not relying on my own perceptions even if they are one-sided and not based in reality.

Seeking answers, I spoke with my high school drama director by phone about my acting prowess, or lack thereof. He assured me that the reason I'd never been cast in a production was not that I didn't have talent. Whew! I was flattered by his encouragement to pursue acting opportunities in college. This was great! However, as he continued, the truth came out.

"If only we had done a play that called for Black cast members," he went on to say. "Something like 'A Raisin in the Sun.' We would have needed even more Black students to fill out the cast, but you would have gotten a part right away."

Devastating. There'd been no chance of being discovered by the college talent scouts in the audience my senior year. By then, I was no longer shy and timid. I was studying classical voice in private lessons, and I was doing quite well. I'd learned to sing, do stage makeup, play in the pit orchestra, as well as many other aspects of live theater, such as running a lighting board. Still, exposure to talent scouts wouldn't have happened unless I was on stage. I pretended to be okay with it because it seemed like my aspirations weren't important to anyone but me, and I didn't want to look like a whiner.

Truth be told, I adored (and still adore) my high school drama director. But he, along with many others in "White America," often did not realize that opportunities are currency, and those of us who are Black lack that currency. Because of our skin, we are relegated to the background in too many situations.

In all of this backstory, I want to make sure you understand that all teenagers are in an awkward stage of life. The hormonal influx and subsequent 'coming of age' process have been tumultuous, exhilarating, and perplexing to the youth that I have taught over the years. I know this was true for me in more ways than one. The truth that adolescent developmental stages can take some youth through very dark places emotionally must ignite a level of compassion in us for our students.

As Christians, we are called to clothe ourselves in Christ. Every day, everywhere, and at all times. As educators clothed in Christ, we consider the needs of our students above our own. Whether in a theater program, a choir, or the classroom, the needs of the students as valued children exceed the importance of the curriculum.

Love must be sincere. Hate what is evil; cling to what is good. Be devoted to one another in love. Honor one another above yourselves.
(Rom. 12:9-10)

CHAPTER 6

GOD-GIVEN GIFTS

*We have different gifts, according to the grace
given to each of us. If your gift is prophesying,
then prophesy in accordance with your faith; if it
is serving, then serve; if it is teaching, then teach;
if it is to encourage, then give encouragement; if
it is giving, then give generously; if it is to lead, do
it diligently; if it is to show mercy, do it cheerfully.
(Rom. 12:6-8)*

My father was an electrical engineer and an intelligent and accomplished man, but everywhere he turned, whether in his own business or while working for others, there were barriers to his success. Even if they were based on his skin color, he questioned himself and his own self-worth. Depression was a part of his life for much of my high school and college years.

Being Black in America can take a toll on a person's psyche. After a year of college at a predominantly White state institution, my academic advisor recommended that I drop out before I flunked out. He cited that 99% of Black women majoring in Engineering fail, so I should "get out now."

I had an ACT composite score of 34 out of a possible 36. I was a member of the National Honor Society, the International Thespian Society, the Varsity Speech and Debate Team (lettering in extemporaneous speaking), and the choir and the orchestra. Despite all of this and being accepted to the engineering program at the state university, because I identified myself as Black on the application, I was automatically placed in a mandatory minority remedial summer program.

My White male academic advisor in Engineering was not shy about the fact that he believed engineering was no place for a woman or a Black person, so it was a big problem for him that I was both of these identifiers. His words stung, which did later motivate me to leave the program at the end of my sophomore year.

The Lord's loving kindnesses indeed never cease,
For His compassions never fail.
They are new every morning; Great is Your
faithfulness. "The Lord is my portion," says my
soul, "Therefore I have hope in Him."
(Lam. 3:22-24 New American Standard Bible)

I was baptized into Christ at the end of my freshman year in 1984, and I was led to minister where God would have me. During my sophomore year, while still pursuing the engineering major, I felt called to education and math. The advisor's words had settled in deep under my skin, and I feared the failure that he'd forecast for me in engineering. The fact that I eventually became a Software Test Engineer and now work as an Engineering Educator is a testament to my God-given gifts in math and science. The setbacks I encountered with my advisor didn't prohibit God's plan for me in Engineering and Education.

I completed a mathematics degree with a focus on applied math and then began the education courses needed for state licensure.

In part, I credit my success in the math program to our department chair – a lovely person and a mathematics education professor who taught me. They were both of European descent, and they encouraged and inspired me to be my best. I knew that they believed in my abilities to do the work and do it well. Because they didn't view my Blackness as a negative, they were the help that I needed to see myself as I should.

However, to the contrary, I had one Black professor in my 4.5 years at the university, and he taught in the education department. He was so thrilled to have a minority in his class that he felt the need to ask if I agreed with his perceptions in every session. His course was Multicultural Diversity in Education, and it was the one course that I truly did not want to attend. He treated me as his sounding board, turning me into the 'other' in class, thus making this one of the worst experiences I had in college other than what my academic advisor had put me through. This professor wasn't looking at my interests above his own. He was seeking validation for his own sake and didn't recognize the disconcerting position he was putting me in.

My advisor taught EG101, a freshman course that presumed prior computer programming experience. I later learned I should have been enrolled in CS101, which was designed for those without that experience and would have met the graduation requirements for my major as well. His blinders against Blackness and females in the field kept him from considering what was the best course for me to take in order to be successful in engineering. I had been admitted to the engineering program, so I qualified to be there. I could have been more successful with the correct guidance. We must take a continual personal inventory of our biases, prejudices, and personal convictions lest they inadvertently influence us. It takes intentionality to remain inspirational and invested in our students. Praying for each student allows the Spirit to reveal their true nature and God-given gifts to us. Once you can see the calling on their lives, share that vision with them. Speak hope into their future. Encourage them to trust in the Lord so that He will make their paths straight.

> Trust in the Lord with all your heart and lean not on your own understanding; in all your ways submit to him, and he will make your paths straight. (Pr. 3:5-6)

CHAPTER 7

UNGODLY THOUGHTS

We demolish arguments and every pretension that
sets itself up against the knowledge of God, and we
take captive every thought to make it obedient to
Christ. (2 Cor. 10:5)

When I worked in a public-school system near D.C., I was on a team of teachers for ninth grade. The team consisted of two math teachers, a social studies teacher, a science teacher, and an English teacher. The five of us shared the same roster of students, which helped us to catch any challenges that our students may have been facing. This was especially helpful if a student was displaying similar academic or behavioral issues in multiple classes. Additionally, the team arrangement allowed us to teach multi-disciplinary units together. One year, in February, during Black History Month, we decided to focus a unit for all of our classes on Black History, culminating in a field trip to the Great Blacks in Wax Museum in Baltimore, MD.

When we completed all the necessary preliminary steps for the field trip, we boarded the bus and were on our way. Entering Great Blacks in Wax, the attendant directed us to the first exhibit, instructing us to proceed from there. My husband had joined us as a chaperone on this trip, and we each had a group of eight students for whom we were responsible. We intended to tour the museum together while keeping track of our sixteen students.

The first exhibit was of a slave ship. It began with a film about slavery watched while sitting in the hull of the mock-up ship. After this, we entered the next room where a naked African woman was displayed, her flesh ripped open from a lashing. Plaques of information about specific slave ships, their captain, and their voyages were interspersed on the walls. There was so much information that my husband and I were caught up reading for much longer than we initially realized.

By the time we turned around, our sixteen students were nowhere to be found. Argh! We walked through the entire museum in search of them only to find them all back on the bus with their headphones on and blank or slightly troubled expressions. We took them to eat before heading back, intending to debrief the trip in earnest the next day.

My colleague who taught Social Studies was also in college earning her Master of Social Work. She was exceptional at speaking with students, aided by her warm and inviting personality. In her classes, she used a technique referred to as Touchstones, which involved sharing and digging deeper into the topic at hand. Applying this, she delved into the impact that the museum had had on each student, considering that they had walked through so quickly and immediately returned to the bus. This seemed to indicate that some emotions had been triggered and needed to be unpacked. Although this teacher was a White woman, neither she nor the rest of our team had previously considered the singular White young man in our group of students.

This poor young man was traumatized to the point of requiring outside counseling. He was so disturbed that he came away with loathing toward himself and all White people, leaving him profoundly depressed about the practice of slavery.

What we as a teaching team had failed to do was prepare the students for the experience in advance. None of them knew what to expect, let alone our sole White student. We didn't even consider this prior to the field trip, but we learned our lesson. I regret the oversight to this day because it reflected a bias for our entire team. That young man was a student whose identity, worth, and value were just as important to preserve as the African-American students who were on that trip.

Although I had grown up in a predominantly White area, I was not prepared for what this young man needed before being confronted with the wax museum. I hadn't yet delved into my views of 'Whiteness' enough to see how my own biases were affecting my willingness to see to the needs of a White student.

I did some soul-searching after that experience and realized that White people were only human and had feelings. I decided that not every White person was consciously choosing to hurt me or, through complicity, condone slavery. Although their humanity was a given, in my upbringing, 'Whiteness' had become synonymous with hatred and inhumanity. My family of origin invoked a sense that all White people held malice toward African-Americans but kept it hidden to avoid being found out by the law.

Unfortunately, the recent resurgence of White Supremacy's public existence supports the belief that there have indeed always been White people around us who have held to those views. They have, perhaps, wished harm to befall me – or my son, family, or friends of African-American heritage – or they possibly would not intervene to stop something bad from happening to us.

It frightens me that I may attend church with, live next door to, or teach with someone who may condone harm inflicted upon myself or my kin because we are Black. I am constantly afraid for my son, who, truthfully, fears for himself as well. When he was in high school, all of us parents of minority students whose sons played basketball together worried about their safety, and it wasn't because they were ever in trouble with the law. We were worried about them 'Driving while Black,' 'Walking while Black,' and 'Being Goofy Teenagers while Black.' The benefit of the doubt is often not extended to Latino, Black, African, or darker-skinned Caribbean males. All of these attitudes and fears filter into the classroom.

There is a constant burden on our personhood and self-concept if we have to stay 'braced for impact' when we walk outside or go to school and encounter White teachers, White parents of classmates, or White coaches or administrators. I felt that pressure throughout middle school, high school, college, and in my adult life as an educator.

It is a weight that minorities carry into your classroom daily, so when you respond with offhandedness or a lack of compassion, or perhaps keep a record of wrongs, or fail to recognize the personhood of the student versus their abilities as a student, it is another negative impact on an already pained psyche.

Do they need to become less sensitive, fearful, and low-grade angry as teens? Yes, they do, but they will learn how to do that from teachers, parents, coaches, and other adults in their orbit as we show them how to frame themselves and their lives in the light of the Gospel of Jesus. As they come to understand that their ultimate worth comes from Him, and not how others view them, there can be less unbridled anger and self-loathing.

> There is no fear in love. But perfect love drives out fear, because fear has to do with punishment. The one who fears is not made perfect in love.
> (1 Jn. 4:18)

They need help to feel secure in their value and their right to exist. All humans matter. The cry of the phrase 'Black Lives Matter' is not to say that White lives do not matter, but instead to say, *please see us and our pain* at the hands of those who are unaware of their Whiteness. They actively hurt us or passively allow injustice at the hands of those who truly believe that 'Whiteness' is superior to 'otherness' and will inflict punishment on us for existing at all.

A famous jazz musician, Al Jarreau, released an album in the 1970s called *We Got By*. Both my mom and dad were into jazz. My dad liked to listen to Nina Simone, and my mom liked to listen to Al Jarreau. One day, I picked up the album cover for Al Jarreau's *We Got By* that was in the cabinet and decided to sit and read the lyrics. I was a teenager. His lyrics for the song "You Don't See Me" struck me between the eyes with its message. A line in the song says, "You don't see me when I'm trying to do right/Maybe you can see me now." The song talks about poverty, the lack of work, and the inability to pay the bills when whatever job he finds requires that he works for "forty hours (which) buys a grocery bag for trash."

His song expressed that pills and needles were all that were the only things available for pleasure. In their poverty, they started stealing, running, and hiding; stealing money, groceries… but wait… they started not caring if they killed someone, if they went to jail, or what might happen to them because they got "so tired of trying to attract your attention/it has occurred to me that you don't see me/you don't wanna see me/I am in your mirror/maybe you can see me now."

Not all of my students were as destitute as this song portrays, but some of them were.

I taught in Ward 8 in Washington, D.C., and some of my students were selling contraband, jumping other students for their iPhones, or jailed for felonies. They were angry and frustrated. "You don't see me when I'm trying to do right [but when I am doing wrong] Maybe you can see me now." We as teachers might be so focused on the flow of the classroom that the agitated, troubled student, who is trying to gain attention, only frustrates and annoys us.

We might feel that we would rather not have them in class. I have been guilty myself of wishing difficult students away, but this song reminds me that they act up simply to be *seen*. They want their challenges to be seen, they want to be known, and, ultimately, they want someone to care enough to help them reach a better place.

At one point in the song, Jarreau sings:

> *"We were walking and*
> *I told you of how my shoes*
> *Of how my shoes were wearing thin*
> *You took your surplus and*

Traded for a favor
Now I'm demented and I'm
Burned unto a cinder
Forty hours buys a grocery
Bag for trash
I took my pistol and I made
Myself a sinner
Will this universe be merciful at last?"

The last line of this stanza asks for mercy. Justice and mercy hang in the balance of our lives because justice addresses the law-breaker with what they deserve for their trespasses, whereas mercy recognizes the trespass but extends grace in the place of complete judgment. It is a difficult balance to find in our lives or our classrooms. We must address challenges with students in our classrooms with mercy and justice in tandem. The most recent movement in schools is called Restorative Justice. Our goal as teachers is to help students grow, both in their knowledge of our subject matter and within their characters. When we are unmerciful or focused only on the trespasses committed in class, we can miss the opportunity to help students become better people. They must learn how and why to change their actions.

Just as we are trying to reach our students, they are also trying to reach us. They are crying out for help, often through aggravating behaviors, and our classroom may be the final place they go for help.

The Lord is good and merciful; our God is so kind. The Lord takes care of helpless people.

I was without help, and he saved me.
(Ps. 116:5-6 Easy-to-Read Version)

There is a phenomenon of 'color blindness' that I have a difficult time understanding. White friends have told me that they grew up being taught that identifying a person's race was bad and that it was better to be 'color blind.' To me, this meant that my differences were discounted, as though it was no different for me living in America than for White Americans; that accessibility to what this country has to offer is the same for everyone. How could this be?

I went in search of further education and insight on 'Whiteness.' I came across "Traces of the Trade: A Story from the Deep North,"[3] about the legacy of slavery in the Northern United States. Descendants of the DeWolf family were gathered by a relative who discovered that the source of their family fortune was rooted in the slave trade that had been run from West Africa to Havana, where enslaved African people worked on sugar cane plantations.

Their masters, the DeWolf family members, hired managers to run their Cuban plantations. Once they harvested the sugar cane, it was shipped to Bristol, Rhode Island, where the DeWolf distillery used the sugar to make rum that was sold in many places, including both Northern and Southern states. At one point, the DeWolf family owned 10,000 enslaved persons.

The documentary follows ten members of this family on a journey to reckon with their ancestors' lives and family business within the slave trade. As I watched, I saw the range of emotions expressed by the family members, and I tried to have empathy for their distress. I admit it was difficult for me as an African-American to feel deep compassion toward them. The fact that it was so challenging showed me that

---

[3]   Traces of the Trade: A Story from the Deep North https://g.co/kgs/qefYDR; See Appendix B

I harbored anger, resentment, and bitterness, which had to be addressed because it grieves the Lord and damages my Christian witness.

I am only human, it is true, but the Lord asks us to set our minds above rather than on earthly things and to rid ourselves of resentment and bitterness. I realized that I had a great deal of healing work to do.

As our nation has journeyed from the Charlottesville Rally where a White young man mentioned on social media that he wanted to smash a Black person's head in to a White supremacists' and Western Chauvinists' insurrection on the U.S. Capitol, we are reminded that there are those that desire the South rise again. The fear of losing position, status, and having Blackness normalized and of equal value to Whiteness is too much for some to bear. Even if our minority and immigrant students were so bold as to grab their worth and value from God, the assault of the community around them, figuratively and physically, would and has threatened to destroy any self-esteem they have.

For some students, the most recent U.S. Capitol insurrection event has created a deeper resolve to be successful and to rise above. In either situation, whether frightened away from trying to succeed or being determined to succeed, as Christian teachers, we are the part of their support system that calls them to seek the Lord's purpose for their lives, regardless of the consequences and the attitudes of the world around them.

And do not grieve the Holy Spirit of God, with whom you were sealed for the day of redemption. Get rid of all bitterness, rage and anger, brawling and slander, along with every form of malice. Be kind and

*compassionate to one another, forgiving each other,
just as in Christ God forgave you. (Eph. 4:30-32)*

*Since, then, you have been raised with Christ, set
your hearts on things above, where Christ is, seated
at the right hand of God. Set your minds on things
above, not on earthly things. For you died, and your
life is now hidden with Christ in God. (Col. 3:1-3)*

Do not repay anyone evil for evil. Be careful to do what is right in the eyes of everyone. If it is possible, as far as it depends on you, live at peace with everyone. Do not take revenge, my dear friends, but leave room for God's wrath, for it is written: "It is mine to avenge; I will repay," says the Lord. On the contrary: "If your enemy is hungry, feed him; If he is thirsty, give him something to drink.

*In doing this, you will heap burning coals on his
head." Do not be overcome by evil, but overcome
evil with good. (Rom. 12:17-21)*

We are called to a higher standard as followers of Christ. On Twitter, there was a young woman who recited why White people ought to be happy that African-American people are not taking revenge. She said if it were up to her, we would make up for the history of wrongs against us going back to slavery.

Although I understand her sentiments, as a Christ-follower I cannot repay evil for evil, even in my heart. I must:

*Cast all [my] anxiety on him because he cares for
[me]. (1 Pet. 5:7)*

Our students could be experiencing the anger and apathy that come from feeling as though things will never change or the depression that can come from being the 'other' so often.

Because one of the fruits of the Spirit is gentleness, we must be gentle with our students as we correct, guide, and at times rebuke them. When we do, we must ask for God's help because He knows our hearts. We fool ourselves with our intentions, but we cannot fool Him. King David said to God:

> Search me, God, and know my heart; test me
> and know my anxious thoughts. See if there is
> any offensive way in me, and lead me in the way
> everlasting. (Ps. 139:23-24)

When we submit ourselves to Him, how we conduct ourselves with our students reflects God's love for them and His glory in our lives. We are His witnesses in this world, and how we live and care for our students speaks volumes to them and their families, not just about ourselves but about our Lord in heaven.

After teaching in the public-school system where most of my students were from underserved populations, I taught in an elite tennis academy and a parochial school where some of my students were White. I was hyperaware of my actions. I constantly asked myself if God would be pleased with how I was treating each of my students.

Some of the adult influences of my youth were extremely Afrocentric, and I felt the need to counter that. To understand identity as God intended, our definitions have to come from the truths in His Word.

Someone who has had a positive impact on me in this area is Joel Freeman, Ph.D. He is an author, lecturer, teacher, and motivational speaker. He has created (and is still creating) material on 'A White Man's Journey through Black History,' as well as an African-American history textbook for high school level. The name of the book is *Black History 365*.

He amazes me because he is a White man who is fascinated by the disingenuous way the history of Black America has been formed and taught in the USA. Again, through his eyes, I have received a different education about 'Whiteness.'

Not ALL White people are unaware of the trauma, the evils, and the irreversible damage done to those of us who hail our heritage from the Transatlantic African Slave Trade, I realized after meeting him. He gives lectures, writes books, speaks to churches, and has made an impact on others in the area of God's view on race. Churches, faith-based Christian organizations, and those of us who live our Christian faith every day need to pursue authentic Christ-like love for others from all languages, tribes, and nations. The Lord's work cannot be done through us when we are not living in submission to Him. His name stands poorly among some Black people in America due to the portrayal of a 'White' Jesus who does not care for the Black man. How He is represented in our lives is how others may receive Him. How is your witness?

Much deep healing is needed. The current climate of racial tension and the hatred that has been inflicted on the families of Breonna Taylor, George Floyd, and many, many others in part due to our 'Blackness' have opened wounds that reveal scars that never truly healed. The belief that they had and everything is okay is 'fake news.'

When 17-year-old Trayvon Martin[4] was shot at point-blank range by neighborhood watchman George Zimmerman, who assumed that Trayvon was stealing from 7-Eleven, I wept for days on end for his family. All Trayvon had in his pockets were Skittles candy and an iced tea that he had paid for and was taking home.

My own son was eleven at that time, but he was getting taller, wearing a men's size 11 shoe, and had dark skin and a penchant for hoodies. I threw his hoodies in the trash can and was terrified every time he wanted to walk a block to the 7-Eleven near our home.

I had nightmares of him being shot for many months, and sometimes I still do, especially since he is now nineteen. He is over 6'2", dark-skinned, with a bass voice and a tendency to be a tad too sarcastic for his own good. He knows that he is a potential target for someone just by existing.

When there was a march on Washington, D.C., led by the Reverend Al Sharpton's organization for change, my son told me that he would not consider going. I was concerned when he responded that way, given that I considered myself an activist of sorts. My mother had participated in boycotts and sit-ins in the 1960s and had been interested in the Black Panther movement of that time period, so activism is somewhat in our blood.

He explained that if someone threw a bottle or there was any kind of unrest, he knew that he would be blamed even though he would not have done anything, simply because he is tall and dark-skinned. He did not want to take the chance. Heartbreaking. Currently, he is a freshman in

---

4   Trayvon Martin's Shooting - Wikipedia - https://bit.ly/3vMWNGO

college and staying as far away as possible from the unrest. I do not blame him.

I bring him up because, as the parent of a young, Black, teenage male, I was fearful. As a teacher, I am aware of the fears my students and their families carry because I also experience them. Teachers need to understand that what happens in the community affects the students and their families. They cannot 'check those emotions at the door,' as much as we may wish they could.

After Shaka died, the students were stunned, confused, and weepy. In the grief training we had at school directly after, I learned that some students would grieve deeply even if they didn't know Shaka because his death could trigger emotions from prior losses they hadn't fully processed. Someone suggested I isolate his desk and make it a place of remembrance for his Geometry classmates. They left him notes and flowers, not wanting anyone else to sit there in any of my other classes because it had been Shaka's desk.

The days following his death were sorrowful for all of us in my classroom. Even with my own heartache, for their sake, I had to be present for them emotionally, although my tears would come from time to time. That was okay, though, because they understood that I was right there with them through it all.

No matter what is going on for us or them, teachers are called to be intentionally present for our students as best we can.

Because I teach in a school of faith, I have the privilege of easily praying with and for my students aloud daily at the start of each class. As I have built a sense of community with certain classes, our prayers have become more personal than just the memorized school prayer.

I have had students ask for prayers for their friends who have been shot, friends who have died due to violence, and those who died or were dying from major illnesses such as cancer. Our students are still learning how to manage their emotions and how to handle grief. They need our example of steadfastness, our compassion, our prayers, and our hope in the Lord to guide them through those challenges.

As Christian educators, we are called to comfort others as we have been comforted by the Lord. The scriptures about comforting others are not meant solely regarding our personal family, friends, or church family, but for all with whom we come into contact, including our students and their families.

All of these experiences have shaped the type of teacher I have become.

CHAPTER 8

QUALIFIED

For this reason, since the day we heard about you, we have not stopped praying for you. We continually ask God to fill you with the knowledge of his will through all the wisdom and understanding that the Spirit gives, so that you may live a life worthy of the Lord and please him in every way: bearing fruit in every good work, growing in the knowledge of God, being strengthened with all power according to his glorious might so that you may have great endurance and patience, and giving joyful thanks to the Father, who has qualified you to share in the inheritance of his holy people in the kingdom of light. (Col. 1:9-13)

I have taught for over twenty years in urban public and parochial schools, a private blended-learning academy, community college, and private academic support institutions. But in the early years of my marriage, I left teaching for a time to pursue a more applicable side of mathematics. During that time, I worked for a NASA government contractor as a software test engineer for shuttle software, for a hospitality company as a software test engineer, as a corporate trainer, and as a technical writer.

When I inevitably returned to my original passion, the classroom, I could answer the question posed every year by some student in a mathematics classroom: What are we *ever* going to use this for? My experiences outside of the classroom helped me develop a broader perspective on how to prepare students for a STEM career and the workplace.

I want to pass on what I have learned because through my varied experiences as a child growing up in a fragmented family, a student, a STEM professional, and an urban teacher, the Lord himself has provided rare lessons. My only hope for this book as I pray over it is that I will be able to encapsulate information that will assist you as a teacher whose faith in Christ Jesus impacts your treatment of your students, the education you provide, and the way you carry yourself.

I believe that there are Biblical principles of love that have been etched into my life by trial-and-error, experience, and prayer that keep me grounded in my teaching and ministry to teenagers.

> Love the Lord your God with all your heart and with all your soul and with all your mind and with all your strength.' The second is this: 'Love your neighbor as yourself.' There is no commandment greater than these. (Mk. 12:30-31)

How do we love the Lord? How do we love our neighbor as ourselves? First of all, I think that we need to define love as God defines it. He says that He is love.

Dear friends, let us love one another, for love comes
from God. Everyone who loves has been born of God
and knows God. Whoever does not love does not
know God, because God is love. (1 Jn. 4:7-8)

In 1 Corinthians 13:1-8, God defines the action of love. Love is a verb, not just an emotion, so we must love both in word and deed. He describes what love is and what it is not.

I could relate to Shaka's pain because of my own suicidal thoughts when I was in high school, so I hurt for him and wished I had reached out in time to help.

When I considered suicide in high school, it was during the most painful time of my life. Leaving for college after a senior year that included rape and sexual assault, I saw myself as being forfeit as a person, so I engaged in promiscuous behaviors (that I dare not explain on paper) for the first semester of my freshman year. During that winter break, I stayed home and mostly slept the days away. When I was awake, I was thinking about how I would commit suicide. *This time,* I thought, *I'll map it out, and it will be perfectly executed.* Instead, when I thought about suicide, the Bible that my grandmother had sent me that September kept coming to mind. It gnawed at me. Maybe I had not tried everything there was to find meaning. Mom's habitual drinking and drug use, as well as Dad's drinking, didn't seem to help them find meaning. I still blamed my rape, in part, on taking the shot of liquor at that party, so I wasn't interested in escaping or seeking meaning by virtue of a substance, even for a moment of respite. But a thought came to me: What if God was real and what if He was eternal?

The only scripture I was familiar with was:

*The Lord is my shepherd, I lack nothing. He makes
me lie down in green pastures, he leads me beside
quiet waters, he refreshes my soul. He guides me
along the right paths for his name's sake. Even
though I walk through the darkest valley, I will fear
no evil, for you are with me; your rod and your staff,
they comfort me. (Ps. 23:1-4)*

This verse hinted to me that if God was eternal and loving, then He was the only One to live for in this life and into eternity. I just wasn't yet convinced that He *was* real or that there was any evidence for His existence, so I continued to plan for suicide. But it was now Plan B.

I returned to college at the end of January for the Spring semester, interested in learning the Bible. I had met someone who worked in the lunch line in our dorm cafeteria. He always had a ready smile. His course of study, Industrial Construction Management (ICM), seemed challenging for him, but he was still a cheerful and inviting young man. An Engineering major myself, I lived on the female wing of the engineering dorm, and we called the male side our 'brother floor.'

My new friend led a Bible study on my 'brother floor.' I began attending weekly that semester while also studying the Bible separately with him and his fiancée between February and May. I began to understand the Bible, how Jesus was a real person and not just a concept, and I made the decision to follow Him for the rest of my life. I was baptized into Christ in May of 1984, and I have never looked back. Through the last three decades, I have only become more convinced of His presence in my life, His eternal existence, and the Holy Spirit's work in the lives of

God's people. Despite this, thoughts of suicide did return to me once more.

In my dad's family, mental health challenges and heavy alcohol consumption have been a mainstay. My father had eight full siblings and two half-siblings, and tragedy in his family was all too common. Of the full siblings, there were five boys and four girls. Mental health issues such as depression, schizophrenia, and suicide have plagued some of my aunts and uncles. Alcohol abuse was an additional curse for Dad's family.

I have battled with depression as well but never called it that. After I found the Lord, I had purpose and direction, so it seemed that depression was behind me. Unwittingly, I became involved with a religious group that had some controlling tendencies. I became trapped in a mentality of people-pleasing where I allowed people who were my age but more advanced in their faith to define my life. I gave them unhealthy access to the boundaries that defined where my relationships with God and others began and ended. As a result, I lost myself by pleasing others, thinking that I was pleasing God. If others were not pleased, God must not be either. This group that I worshipped with were all in their 20s, and they lived by perfectionistic ideals for worship and behaviors. They even had rules for how others' bodies should be presented. I wanted the honor bestowed upon leaders, so I adopted harsh tactics for correcting others if they weren't behaving as per the standards of Christ, in my estimation. I evangelized and tried to draw many people in, but only to show how spiritual and connected I was to God. I had the Holy Spirit on speed dial, I thought, and all was well.

I was focused on bringing as many guests as possible to Bible study, an action that was praised heavily by those in our campus ministry. Although I was inviting people, for weeks I couldn't report any visitors, which made me look like a pretty bad Christian to those I was trying to impress. I felt that my value was diminishing as we were demoted or promoted based on our ability to bring in new converts. One week, I thought I'd have a visitor that I'd invited, but she told me just before Bible study that she couldn't make it. I whined and begged for her to come. She responded, "You don't care about me, but only about me coming to your Bible study. I am never coming now!" When I showed up again without a visitor, I was looked down on. I began to reconsider suicide. I was clearly a bad Christian and a lousy person who didn't deserve to live.

I was weeping so loudly in my dorm room that my roommate told me she could hear me down the hall. She told me that people with faith do not cry that way and to "snap out of it, for heaven's sake." About two weeks later, I met a Christian who was visiting our campus from another campus ministry. We had lunch together and discussed some of his observations about the campus ministry movement based on his experiences. Illumination. The insensitive, controlling nature of our group was not unique to us, and the pain and despair I was feeling were not unique to me. I believe that God sent this young man to 'snap me out of my depression,' not because his words were prophetic but because his love for the Lord revealed God's truth. God's love provides the basis for self-concept and self-love; because He loved us, we can then love others. We don't need to reach out to others to earn God's love. He's already given it to us.

*For God so loved the world that he gave his one
and only Son, that whoever believes in him shall not
perish but have eternal life. (Jn. 3:16)*

What I did not realize was, once I became a Christian, I was already qualified in His eyes and given worth by Him. Pleasing others is not part of His plan. It is only about living a life worthy of His calling.

One high school student who had been attending our congregation was from Mexico and spoke Spanish. My Spanish is much better now, but back then, I needed to improve, so I was eager to converse with her. She was a patient soul, encouraging me even though I spoke slowly. She was happy that I wanted to learn her language.

It was great fun for me, and she enjoyed my company. She had epilepsy and lived in extreme poverty with a mom who drank too much and two much younger siblings. She was struggling in her senior year of high school and in danger of not graduating because she refused to learn textbook English and was failing her English course. She felt that her conversational English was enough to get by. Truthfully, I believe that she needed an Individualized Education Program (IEP), but she did not have one, so two others and I tutored her to help her pass her English class.

My college Bible study leader encouraged me to share the Bible with her and she was baptized into Christ at the age of nineteen, which was awesome. After she graduated, she had to address many challenges, from her health to her living conditions. In addition to her mother and young siblings, she had a brother who was a 'big time' traveling drug dealer who sold in multiple states and a stepdad from Mexico who was frequently deported.

For her eleventh birthday, her brother gave her PCP, which led to an overdose. She believed that this caused her to develop epilepsy, a condition she had not previously had. She was hospitalized and spent a few months in a psychiatric ward before she was able to return home. She lived with epilepsy for the rest of her life.

When she lived with her mom, I would pick her up for worship services. At the church building, people would complain to me about her body odor, insisting that I talk to her about it. Truthfully, hygiene was a real problem for her.

The issue mainly stemmed from big cockroaches in the bathroom at her home, making her afraid to take a shower. Most people at the church were either unaware of or insensitive to her personal challenges. Often, our perceptions are filtered through our own experiences, so if we are aware of our cleanliness, we assume anyone would be aware of their body odor and able to do something about it. Godliness requires compassion and kindness, though. It was difficult to watch people's attitudes toward her. Often, she did not take her medications because she didn't like how they made her feel. Sometimes that negligence resulted in seizures during the service. Others would tell me that she refused to take her medication to garner sympathy and attention from others because of her seizures. Their assumptions led to criticism and anger from feeling manipulated. Although the medication was an issue, she also needed therapy to address an incredibly dysfunctional and ungodly home life.

The LORD preserves the simplehearted; I was
helpless, and He saved me.
(Ps. 116:6 Berean Study Bible)

Her stepfather was regularly deported but always found a way back, putting their family in a constant state of high alert. Moving out on her own would free her of that and establish independence, we thought. So, we helped her with the forms for Social Security Disability Insurance (SSDI), which she qualified for and received, giving her the necessary monetary assistance.

With help from others in the church, she moved from her mom's trailer to one of her own. She began keeping herself clean, taking her epilepsy medication, and even helped her family when she could. Everything looked great, and she remained positive.

During Spring Break, I received a phone call from a friend who informed me that there had been a fire in her trailer. Apparently, she had turned on the gas oven for heat, and the pilot light went out. When it came back on, the gas the trailer had filled with ignited. Having epilepsy and no fresh air caused her to have a grand mal seizure, such as she'd, unfortunately, experienced in my car once.

The flames became obvious, and the firefighters were called, but they found it difficult to open the door because she had fallen right behind it. She was lovingly chubby. By the time they were able to pry the door open, she had inhaled too much smoke, and the heat from the flames had caused her body to swell. She was pronounced dead on the scene. I was heartbroken.

Her family had no money for the funeral, let alone a burial, so our church held the funeral for free. We put jars in all of the 7-Elevens in town (as well as other stores that allowed us) to collect donations for her burial.

All the while, I agonized about her faith. Was it enough? What did God have in mind for her?

On the day of the funeral, her mom wanted an open casket. The bloated body did not look like her at all. She was not the young lady I remembered. I pondered that at twenty-two years old. It was the first time I had considered that what you see is not all there is to a person. Her personality, her warmth, and her spirit were gone, leaving only the body. I concluded that perhaps we are more than what is seen. Our soul and spirit are housed in this body, but it's a temporary tent, and we are more than that. The same is true of the students whose souls I would eventually minister to in the classroom.

> *For we know that if the earthly tent we live in is destroyed, we have a building from God, an eternal house in heaven, not built by human hands. Meanwhile we groan, longing to be clothed instead with our heavenly dwelling, because when we are clothed, we will not be found naked. For while we are in this tent, we groan and are burdened, because we do not wish to be unclothed but to be clothed instead with our heavenly dwelling, so that what is mortal may be swallowed up by life. Now the one who has fashioned us for this very purpose is God, who has given us the Spirit as a deposit, guaranteeing what is to come. (2 Cor. 5:1-5)*

CHAPTER 9

THE GATEKEEPER

The one who enters by the gate is the shepherd of
the sheep. The gatekeeper opens the gate for him,
and the sheep listen to his voice. He calls his own
sheep by name and leads them out.
(Jn. 10:2-3)

As teachers, we are gatekeepers, according to the Mental Health & Suicide Prevention Lifeline and stated in the guideline: "People in a community who have face-to-face contact with large numbers of community members as part of their usual routine; they may be trained to identify people at risk of suicide and refer them to treatment or supporting services as appropriate." https://suicidepreventionlifeline. org/mental-health-suicide-prevention-glossary/

"In 2017, there were more than 6,200 suicide deaths among adolescents and young adults ages 15-24, making it the second-leading cause of death for that age group."

As Christian teachers, we are faith gatekeepers. We open the gate for the Good Shepherd to enter into the sheep pen. He calls His sheep by name, and they follow. Our hope and prayer are that they will follow the Shepherd and come to hear His voice because we love them with His love.

I continue to mourn Shaka's passing. This, along with the deaths of others whose lives were cut short by tragedy or their own hand, has taught me empathy through grief and changes how I relate to my students and even my own children.

As of the writing of this book, it has been thirty-three years since Shaka's death, and I still tear up when I think of him. He died at the age of sixteen during the early days of the first quarter of his junior year, so he is heavy on my heart during the first nine weeks of every school year. I consider what his life and death continue to mean to me as a teacher and in my constant transformation, which involves re-evaluating and shifting my mindset regarding the purpose of being an educator.

A Bachelor of Science in Mathematics, certifications in engineering education, teaching licensure for 7-12 grade Mathematics, and training in STEM educational leadership have given me a career. However, my mission is to positively affect the hearts and souls of my students as a result of the love that God has shown to me. My greatest desire is to show each student how valuable they are in God's eyes and mine. Their value and worth have been established by the One who created them, and these are not based on how well they understand Geometry, Engineering, or any other subject.

Seeking to enter the heart and pain of Shaka's life and seeing him not as a challenging math student but a young person in need of support, guidance, love, inspiration, and encouragement was my greater mission and purpose.

When I finally glimpsed this mission during parent-teacher conference week, I was a day too late to make a difference in Shaka's life. However, the impact that he has on my life and teaching everyday keeps him alive in me.

No one can control another person's decisions, and even if I had been timelier, it may have made no difference for Shaka but I continue to think that perhaps it would have. However, I do believe that, as teachers who have faith in Christ Jesus, our focus should be on the class subject matter in the context of the student as a whole person. They are made in God's image and becoming, evolving, and changing into an adult. We are called to support them with guidance, love, and inspiration in the schema of teaching in our Christian faith.

However, we cannot do that if we are not being continually filled with and by the Holy Spirit and constantly striving to nurture a growing relationship with our Lord. We need to know that we are loved and cherished by the Almighty and thereby filled with His tenderness and compassion. Our service to students is borne out of the overflow of our love for Christ and His love for us.

Kindness toward those in our care is one of the greatest gifts we can give. If we mess up or are having an off day, an apology to students for an abrupt nature goes a long way toward developing a supportive relationship with a student.

CHAPTER 10

PAIN AS A TEACHER

*Who is the man that fears the LORD? Him shall He
teach in the way He chooses.*
(Ps. 25:12 New King James Version)

My husband and I adopted two infant children who
are three and a half years apart in age. Our oldest
child, Gina, was placed with us for adoption at six months
old. She was (and is) adorable, with an infectious laugh,
attractive features, and a loving and lovable personality.
When Gina was about two years old, we fostered siblings
who were seven and eight. By the time they came to us,
they had been in foster care for five years. They seemed like
nice children, calling us 'Mom' and 'Dad' the first day they
met us. I later learned this is usually a sign of grief.

When they moved in, Gina shared a room with the
girl, who was the eldest, and the boy had his own room.
Many challenging situations arose with these children as
a result of their family of origin and the foster homes they
had lived in. As time went on, I hoped that providing them

love and attention would be enough to turn the tide of rage, sleeplessness, and the inappropriate behaviors they exhibited. Although I tried to be what they needed, they quickly became more than we could handle.

My love was not enough. Gina bore the brunt of the unrest in our home and the chaos of emotions flowing like tumultuous waves each day. At the time, I was a full-time homemaker. Although this was initially due to Gina's health, I expected it to be a benefit for the two foster children as well. However, without additional support during the day, I found that I was being poured out like wine. Trying to be everything was leaving me with nothing. My husband and I were concerned that we might not be equipped to address their multi-faceted issues. We considered ending the pre-adoptive fostering arrangement.

In the fostering and adoption community, there is a great deal of stigma on what is called a 'disruption.' This is when potential adoptive parents choose not to adopt their pre-adoptive foster child(ren). But after two inpatient psychiatric care stays, a call to the police, and an episode when the boy attempted to stab me with a butcher knife, I concluded that I could not withstand the arrangement as it was any longer. However, I wouldn't do as their grandmother had done, leaving them on the steps of Child Protective Services with their clothing in a garbage bag. The least we could do was show kindness as we waited for CPS to relocate them to a therapeutic foster home. We prayed for and with them and considered how we could continue to bless them.

We had discovered that the boy was envious of Gina having a family, and his grief made him determined to harm her. Additionally, there was ample evidence of many other challenges that were not in the children's background paperwork, which we were not trained or capable enough to handle, especially with our sickly two-year-old.

We had planned a trip to Disney World for the whole family, and although a therapeutic foster home had been found, we took them on the trip anyway. About a week after we returned, the social worker arrived to relocate them to their new home.

That day was emotionally brutal for all of us. They cried, we cried, and the little girl tried to barricade herself in the bedroom closet. Despite our heartache, we felt it was kinder to accept that our home was not what they needed. Healing would be a lifelong endeavor for them, and they needed an environment where they could thrive. Not only that, we had to be considerate of Gina's needs and the potential danger of having them stay, given the threatening behaviors the little boy displayed toward her in the nine months they were with us. It was clear they needed to move on.

Kindness requires being friendly, generous, and considerate – in short, a deliberately thoughtful act in consideration of what is best for someone else. This act of kindness was one of the most difficult things we have ever done for our family.

CHAPTER 11

DO NOT HINDER

People were also bringing babies to Jesus for him to place his hands on them. When the disciples saw this, they rebuked them. But Jesus called the children to him and said, "Let the little children come to me, and do not hinder them, for the kingdom of God belongs to such as these. Truly I tell you, anyone who will not receive the kingdom of God like a little child will never enter it." (Lk. 18:15-17)

When Gina was four years old, not knowing I was observing, she placed a random shoebox onto our front yard. I had no idea why; I thought perhaps it was a home for her doll or some other plaything since she was a curious and creative little one. As darkness overcame the skies, I went out to the yard, collected the toys, and shooed her into the house with her dolls. Only then did I look in the shoebox, realizing it was heavier and more unbalanced than I'd expected. I remember an apple, a toy from McDonald's, and several other items rolling around inside the box. Bewildered, I asked her what the collection meant. She replied that she left the box for any poor or hungry children who might wander by to have something to eat and toys to play with.

The humorous but sweet thing about her four-year-old thought was that we live in a cul-de-sac of a middle-class neighborhood, so it wasn't likely that a hungry child would wander down our street. It is definitely the thought that counts. Her sensitive spirit remains, and I still call on her to serve with me at homeless shelters or to collect non-perishable items for our school's Thanksgiving food drive.

Gina grew up with severe, life-threatening allergies, asthma, dyslexia, and a manual dexterity issue due to a birth injury, but she weathered these challenges like a trooper. With child-like faith, she believed God would help her, and I believe He did. She is now twenty-two and still struggles with asthma, allergies, and other ailments that annoy her from time to time. I thank God for her every day because, at seventeen, she wanted to choose the same path as Shaka, but we still have the gift of her in our lives.

I thought she was happy because she was always cheerful until I caught her at the age of fourteen using scissors to cut her thigh as part of her ritual to help deal with stress. 'Cutting' is the term used in therapy, and apparently, it can be common in girls, starting at age ten. I had thought I was protecting her from difficulties, taking care of her health and well-being, and doing all I could do.

Do you hear the common thread between this story, the situation with our foster children, and my experience with Shaka? My goal was to create a good life with a fun family. We took numerous vacations: We went to Disney World twice (once was after I'd been diagnosed with a life-threatening illness, yet I traveled for their sake); to Six Flags America in Maryland and Six Flags Great Adventure in New Jersey; and enjoyed annual vacations staying in condos or villas. Gina's upbringing was documented with memory albums, photoshoots, and life books, proving how dedicated I was to her quality of life, despite her chronic illnesses.

Yeah, still about me, not really about her in the end. I had something to prove to myself about my worth as a person. I wanted to be her savior. I attached my value to her as her mother. It was subtle at first, but eventually, I began to see how I depended on her for my worth.

Cutting was the most confusing, alarming, and seemingly purposeless and destructive action I had ever seen. Why would you purposely injure yourself? I asked this question of her, in online support chat rooms, to fellow colleagues who were counselors, and to anyone else I thought could help. I read up on the practice. We sought therapy. I gained insight from one of my counselor colleagues, who had also been a 'cutter' in high school. My dreams for Gina and what she could become didn't include this detour. Therapy helped, and my colleague also helped Gina, who knew her from the school she attended, which was also where we worked. I was just starting to breathe again when she told me one year over Christmas break that she was having thoughts of harming herself.

I called the suicide prevention hotline, and they advised me to take her to the emergency room right away. I piled her into the car, and we drove to the Children's National Medical Center in D.C. We were taken to a triage area and then given a room. I did not know how to feel, what to do, or how to process the situation. Fear constricted my breathing. The room had a bed, a recliner, and a TV tuned to the Disney Channel. I tried to behave as though this was normal. "Look! Let's watch Phineas and Ferb," I suggested lightly. All the while, I was stunned, confused, scared – so very scared, and feeling very alone.

A nurse asked to speak to Gina alone to determine what needed to be done next. I hoped they would offer medication for her previous diagnoses of ADHD, depression, and anxiety. Maybe they would just keep her overnight. *Yeah, I am okay with that,* I thought. However, after speaking with Gina, the nurse was convinced that she could and would harm herself, so she needed inpatient care.

My heart was laid bare by the circumstances. I was desperate for God's kindness, patience, and peace, so I cried out to Jesus to show me what Gina needed from me in that moment. I surrendered to the realization that none of this was in my control.

She was taken to a ward where she had to stay for at least a week. She'd be reassessed at that time, and we would find out if her length of stay would be extended. We were only able to speak with her on the phone once a day for the first few days before visitation was allowed. One of my teacher colleagues whom Gina had bonded with at school went to see her then. Her presence was a breath of fresh air for Gina and our whole family. Her visit encouraged Gina's spirit, and she prayed with and continued to pray for Gina. I am forever grateful for my colleague's kindness and ministry.

Despite being uplifted myself by my colleague's visit, I remained numb for most of the week. When they were ready to discharge her, we had a family therapy session. It was brutally difficult to endure because of what we learned about Gina and the implications that were leveled at us about our parenting.

This session was the first of many over the next two years. We learned about all of the behaviors she had been hiding and all of the ways she tried to be the 'good' girl we wanted while masking a very different persona. It didn't help that my husband was always involved in church leadership, so she considered herself a preacher's kid with impossible expectations.

We had high hopes for her, but we were not seeing the reality she lived growing up. She is in college now and still searching for her purpose, as many of us do in our early twenties. We had hindered her in ways that we didn't understand and still do not fully grasp.

When Gina was almost four years old, we adopted a son. Recently, when our son turned seventeen, we found out about unwanted activities that he had been participating in. Both my husband and I have grieved the loss of our unrealistic dreams for our teens but accept that some of the hindrances in their lives were based on our expectations.

Our solace is that we have sowed precious seeds from God into their lives. I have now laid both of my children at the altar before God. I truly have to do this in my heart daily to keep anxiety and fear from controlling how I interact with them. They love us, and our relationships are healthy and intact. We are eternally grateful to the Lord for those relationships.

Parents are their children's first teachers, and with our actions, we teach them that they are loved and how to love others. We are not asked to do this with perfection, nor could we, but in striving for intentionality as we are called to be the 'light of the world,' how much more so should we be one of God's lights to our children.

You are the light of the world. A town built on a hill
cannot be hidden. Neither do people light a lamp
and put it under a bowl. Instead they put it on its
stand, and it gives light to everyone in the house.
(Matt. 5:14-15)

The journey with my own children has been challenging. If not for the kindness of teachers, counselors, a dearly loved principal, and coaches, who were my comrades in arms, navigating the tumultuous seas of child-rearing would have been even more difficult. This 'village' aimed for the same goal of directing their hearts and souls toward the positive love of God. Our family got to be at the receiving end of what I am writing about.

Those of us who work with young people need to be involved in ministering to their hearts in an up-close and personal way for them to move into adulthood and not be caught in arrested development as an adolescent. Absorbing a God-fearing, kind, and loving environment as they mature will prepare them to become even more than they believed they could as God's loving-kindness causes growth, even when it is borne of adversity or pain.

Therefore, as God's chosen people, holy and dearly
loved, clothe yourselves with compassion, kindness,
humility, gentleness and patience. (Col. 3:12)

We lived in malice and envy, being hated and hating
one another. But when the kindness and love of God
our Savior appeared, he saved us, not because of
righteous things we had done, but because of his
mercy. (Tit. 3:3-5)

CHAPTER 12

LOVE IS PATIENT

Be joyful in hope, patient in affliction,
faithful in prayer.
(Rom. 12:12)

Defining 'patience' requires us to define the word 'forbearance' since, in many translations of the scriptures, these two words seem to be interchangeable. According to Google Dictionary, *forbearance* means 'patient self-control, restraint, and tolerance,' while *patience* is 'the capacity to accept or tolerate delay, trouble, or suffering without getting angry or upset.'

Throughout our twenty-eight years of marriage, my husband and I have been surrogate parents to twelve teens; four did not live with us, but the other eight did. We were a host family to six students who were pursuing professional tennis or hoping to attend a university through a tennis scholarship. The other two teens were high school students who were escaping volatile family situations. In both of those situations, their families allowed us to be part of the solution to their challenges.

With their troubled circumstances, neither of these young people was in a healthy frame of mind when they entered our home, which impacted us as well for a time. One had been involved in an unhealthy relationship that became violent, but she continued to be drawn to the abusive individual. My husband consulted his mother, a godly woman who urged us to be patient in love and continue to remind this young lady of her value in the eyes of the Lord. Eventually, after many conversations with her about her worth, she initiated the end of the relationship. We rejoiced in this great milestone, but her abuser did not leave without harming her one last time. She ended up in the ER with severed tendons in one hand after being on the losing end of a tug-of-war. She was tussling with the abuser when he released her from his grip in such a way that she fell through the glass pane of a storefront window with explosive energy.

We did not find out about the incident until we arrived to pick her up from a friend's house and saw the cast encasing her hand and wrist with her arm in a sling. She required restorative surgery to reattach the tendons in her hand. She remained in our home throughout the entire ordeal. In occupational therapy, her goals included full range of motion in her hand and the ability to make a tight fist easily. I prayed that her assailant would not win by leaving her with a handicap. She had occupational therapy three times per week while continuing to attend the high school where I taught at the time. She hated occupational therapy because she had to move her hand in ways that were painful. Those movements were necessary to keep the scar tissue from causing permanent damage that would limit her function. The rehabilitation process was not simple or short-lived, and there came a time when the injury, rehabilitation, and her family of origin converged in ways that were interruptions to the healing process.

On Memorial Day weekend, while we were visiting family, it became obvious that there would be a reckoning, if you will. Our challenge was that when we authorized her surgery, my husband signed the financial forms instead of listing the young woman's mother. We were sued by the surgeon for the fees, and we had a frustrating phone confrontation with her family.

On the Monday of that holiday weekend, we were going to pick her up after 5 PM from where she was hanging out with her family of origin to bring her back for school on Tuesday. When we called to set the pick-up time, her family confronted us with objections. They said that school could wait and we should let her stay for at least another day. Now, in our family, the rule was that unless you were sick, you were getting up and going to school. So, we drove up there anyway to get her and then had a heart-to-heart with her when we got home.

We explained that while her family was not irresponsible for wanting her to take an extra day or two away from school, in our home, we live by a different rule. If she wanted to stay with us, she would have to abide by our rules in our house, not her family's. She chose to live with her family. Although she had originally moved in with us so she could graduate from her previous school, she decided it was more desirable to live with them even if she had to change schools.

It was years later when she called to express her appreciation for the help and the healing, along with letting me know that she had come to know the Lord. We had prayed for her to be awakened to the Lord's presence all the days that she was in our home, but at the time, she seemed to have no interest or willing participation in attending worship services. The Lord works wonders in the lives of young people when we invest in loving them as God loves. When we tune in and surrender to Him in His leading, He teaches us how to love deeply and sacrificially.

The other young person's story was similar. A teen from church was feeling rejected and disassociated from a family that was in angst at the time, and we offered our home as a respite to her. This young lady's distress manifested in troubling behaviors when she was in our home that impacted me personally on several levels. We had to make some tough decisions, and she and her family worked through difficult issues for her to be able to return home. Many years later, I was contacted by this individual, now a grown adult. She thanked us and updated us on her life's accomplishments. She wanted to be a foster parent herself as a result of the time she spent with us. Many more years later, during orientation week at the high school where I teach, I heard my name called. It was the same 'grown adult,' now enrolling her 9th-grade son in the school.

It was a pleasant reunion only because the Lord had given my husband and me extra measures of patience. I had been hurt and angered by some of the decisions she made when she was living with us. I needed to forgive her and let go in the name of the patience of God. Being patient in affliction demonstrates God's love to others. The outcome of that patience was genuine reconciliation. Now, I am close to her son, who graduated high school and is attending college. How great is the love of God!

See what great love the Father has lavished on us,
that we should be called children of God!
And that is what we are! (1 Jn. 3:1)

There was a situation about two years ago involving a student who was regularly rude to me. My school had an advisory period that many upperclassmen resented, and they whined about the work designed to be completed during this period. This particular young lady often spoke negative and mean things about advisory and me when I tried to enforce the rules concerning this period. As a junior, she was quite difficult to work with. She was again in my advisory period during her senior year; however, she was kind and pleasant to be around. I asked her about the change in her behavior, and she informed me that she'd been mean to a lot of her teachers, but it had not been personal; she was just going through 'something.'

I try to remember the situations with the surrogate teen relationships that I have spoken about so that I am not personalizing everything, which is something I fall into easily. Personalizing makes it about people accepting me rather than relying on God to reveal His perspective of the student. Instead of being the light of God's love, I become focused on myself and how they hurt me. My need for affirmation takes over, then fear of being a failure as a teacher, then anger grips me, and this slippery slope takes me into a pit of defeat. Patient self-control, restraint, and tolerance for our young people are required to stay out of the 'defeated teacher' pit.

Individualized Education Plans (IEPs) are created to address and compensate for health impairments and other barriers that impact a student's ability to navigate the traditional classroom instruction methods and environment. They are based on neuropsychological and other evaluations to provide these students the best opportunity for learning without unnecessary obstacles.

I didn't realize that I could benefit from having an IEP for myself. I was unaware of the issue that caused me to struggle. Let me explain. Although I have taught Geometry, it was my own worst subject as a student. These days, technologically, there are a great deal of helpful tools that allow visualization of objects in three dimensions. However, in 1981, the only assistance I received for seeing objects in 3D was a series of dashed lines strategically placed to indicate the hidden edge of an object such as a pyramid. The trouble was, I still only saw lines on a page, with one of them being dashed. I did not see three dimensions at all. Visual puzzles where you could view them from a certain angle to produce a 3D image never worked for me. Later, I learned that I had poor depth perception that caused me to struggle with spatial relationships. I also learned that this was a common challenge in women and one of the reasons men in STEM fields often disparaged women's aptitude for math. My lack of depth perception also wreaked havoc with learning to parallel park, but I digress.

The whole 3D section of Geometry was a bust for me, and I thought definitely, without a doubt, I was really dumb. Everyone else seemed to be getting it, so what was *my* problem? I went to my Geometry teacher to ask her for help. She broke a sweat trying to explain it to me, but I just did not 'see' what she 'saw' in the diagrams at all. That quarter was the first time I ever got a D on a report card. I was mortified and self-deprecating because of it. It never occurred to me that there could be a type of visualization I simply didn't have and something about which I could not have done anything. I would have needed physical models of the objects to 'see' what everyone else already 'saw.'

My daughter, Gina, attended a Montessori school from when she was three until she was about seven. Montessori school theory involves spans of time for cognitive and behavioral development. Growing children reach milestones at different ages than their same-aged counterparts, so different planes of development have a built-in fluidity. I was amazed at this educational theory and took it to heart.

In pre-k and kindergarten, Gina was curious about quite a few of the 'works' in the Montessori classroom, but she avoided anything that had to do with letters or numbers. It became obvious she had not reached all of the developmental milestones to be able to move on to primary school – or the equivalent of first grade. We let her stay another year, thinking she could traverse the developmental hurdle, given more time.

However, she still resisted the 'sandpaper letters' work with intentionality, and upon realizing how hard she worked to circumvent interacting with letters, her concerned teacher alerted us. I began to wonder if Gina would benefit from an IEP.

Meanwhile, there were other challenges that Gina was struggling with. She had difficulty tying her shoes, but we adapted by using Velcro. She also had trouble with buttons and zippers – and anything that required fine motor skills.

In time, we thought it was important to move her up to the primary level of the Montessori school. Her teacher was a reading specialist who became concerned over Gina's inability to recognize shapes, letters, and numbers.

To compound matters, Gina had been born with a lifeless left arm, so she was in physical therapy to increase sensation and movement with her arm and hand. Now that she was older, we employed occupational therapy to improve her functional abilities.

During her occupational therapy evaluation, the therapist explained to me that Gina had bilateral integration dysfunction. During birth, the neural pathways in her left arm were injured (known as a Brachial-Plexus injury); therefore, her frontal lobe, which typically would process the input and help coordinate her bilateral movements, was impacted. The lack of clarity caused by her underdeveloped neurological pathways created chaos for her with processing and responding to fine motor tasks such as zippers, buttons, and shoelaces, as well as being able to recognize shapes, letters, and numbers. She was diagnosed with dyslexia (letters) and dyscalculia (numbers). Gina needed to be taught how to use both sides of her body in tandem, so we enrolled her in karate, piano lessons, dance, and other activities that encouraged bilateral coordination. As a result, her functional skills with buttons, zippers, and tying laces, as well as her ability to read, showed tremendous improvement.

Gina's journey was difficult for the whole family. The challenges of dyslexia and dyscalculia don't resolve and will remain a part of her for the remainder of her life.

The students in our classes who have IEPs or whom you suspect may need an IEP are not being difficult for the fun of it. If they cannot decipher what you are writing, or their sentence structure indicates a poor command of the English language despite their age, or math symbols or logic are causing a great deal of frustration – this should raise a flag of concern for you, as a teacher. Again, instead of plowing ahead and staying focused on getting through your content, take time to send an email or call the parent, alert your academic intervention specialist or a guidance counselor, and talk directly to the student about their challenges. Doing this will show them that you have a genuine concern for their well-being and ability to grasp the material.

I have had colleagues who berated children for not putting sentences together well. Perhaps they needed private tutoring or a neuropsychological evaluation to determine if there was something more going on than just poor grammar. Maybe their family traveled during their elementary years, and they missed the basics. Either way, vilifying the student out of exasperation does not help them and is not loving.

Additionally, if the student does have an IEP and you don't know how to provide adequate accommodation for your course, don't ignore the IEP or panic, assuming it will be too much work. Instead, ask the special education specialist for assistance. I also recommend reading an educational publication or watch a video on the topic. In short, educate yourself so that you can be God's light and love to that child, for their sake as well as your own.

Gina's IEP helps her in college as well because dyslexia, dyscalculia, and her challenges with her left arm and hand are permanent. They are a part of her. She will learn to navigate these challenges, but she can always benefit from additional resources along the way. Be understanding to your students. A student with a need for additional resources does not want to be different from their peers. Show compassion and be an ally: for them and their family. No one wants to watch their child suffer or be unable to complete assignments based on factors they can't control, so having an ally is water to a thirsty soul.

Realize that an IEP may not even be enough. In Gina's case, it was not. There were occupational therapy appointments three times a week for years, private tutors, and wonderful teachers who dedicated extra time with her. It is hard work supporting a child who needs additional resources. As teachers, let's not make their lives more difficult by being unwilling to figure out how to modify lessons when necessary.

The truth is, often modifications that benefit one student will help all of the students and create an opportunity for increased comprehension of your lesson. Love is kind and patient and is not self-seeking. The end result should be the well-being of the student, sought with patience and understanding.

> *Whoever welcomes one of these little children in*
> *my name welcomes me; and whoever welcomes me*
> *does not welcome me but the one who sent me.*
> *(Mk. 9:37)*

CHAPTER 13

REJOICE WITH THE TRUTH

*Love does not delight in evil but rejoices
with the truth. (1 Cor. 13:6)*

Students with troubled souls can often be incredibly
challenging to teach. They seek attention in ways that
distract and detract from instruction as they focus on
getting someone to make them feel visible and important.

In high school, I was definitely a troubled soul. My
family of origin is as fragmented as many of my own
students' families. My parents divorced and remarried,
bringing step-siblings – who are now ex-step-siblings
because that marriage also ended. Being African-American
and born in 1965 to a mom who was an activist, I learned
that some saw being Black as a negative. Still, I did not
completely understand this until I moved in with my
father and stepmom. They lived in a state with a Black
population of only 4.12%. The Ku Klux Klan and other
White Supremacy groups met regularly in rallies or church
buildings that supported Neo-Nazism or Aryanism.

I attended a predominantly White state university where African-Americans now make up 2.4% (640 out of 25,000 students on campus) of the population, but when I attended – majoring in Math – African-Americans comprised only 1% (250 out of 25,000) of the student population. Being raised in Washington D.C. during grade school, I still visited annually to stay with my mother, per the custody agreement. Because of this, I was able to experience a great deal of African-American culture during these stays. I returned to my Alma Mater each Fall to be treated as 'other': misunderstood, defined, and accused of many things based solely on caricatures or stereotypes that those in my university and even my church family held close to their hearts as truths.

The result of that pain and the 'felt' and 'perceived' neglect of my family of origin was that I craved validation, kindness, recognition, hope, inspiration, and love. Before finding my church family and faith, I looked for love in all the wrong ways and all the wrong places. Even when I found faith, I did not know how to 'know' His love. Because Paul prays:

> For this reason I kneel before the Father, from whom every family in heaven and on earth derives its name. I pray that out of his glorious riches he may strengthen you with power through his Spirit in your inner being, so that Christ may dwell in your hearts through faith. And I pray that you, being rooted and established in love, may have power, together with all the Lord's holy people, to grasp how wide and long and high and deep is the love of Christ, and to know this love that surpasses knowledge—that you

may be filled to the measure of all the fullness of
God. (Eph. 3:14-19)

I realize now that through prayer and supplication, the ability to truly know His love is gifted to us by the Almighty.

The result of not 'knowing' His love and my insecurity as His child was that I looked throughout the church for those who would inspire me, who cared and would listen, and when I found them, I would magnify them to positions of authority and power in my life that belong only to God the Father. When they failed me, as people inevitably do, I would crumble or wish ill on their lives, although it was not their fault that I deified them in the first place and demoted God, as far as influence and self-definition were concerned.

It is a wonderful truth that Jesus has pity on us because we are but sheep without a shepherd.

When Jesus landed and saw a large crowd, he had
compassion on them, because they were like sheep
without a shepherd. So he began teaching them
many things. (Mk. 6:34)

It has been an important realization that I am a sheep. When I found faith, I needed a shepherd, and I sought out shepherds within the church. The word 'shepherd' has been used as a synonym for 'overseer' to describe an elder in the church. I looked to my peers to meet my needs instead of the Good Shepherd.

Very truly I tell you Pharisees, anyone who does not
enter the sheep pen by the gate, but climbs in by
some other way, is a thief and a robber. The one who

enters by the gate is the shepherd of the sheep. The gatekeeper opens the gate for him, and the sheep listen to his voice. He calls his own sheep by name and leads them out. When he has brought out all his own, he goes on ahead of them, and his sheep follow him because they know his voice. (Jn. 10:1-4)

Therefore Jesus said again, "Very truly I tell you, I am the gate for the sheep. All who have come before me are thieves and robbers, but the sheep have not listened to them. I am the gate; whoever enters through me will be saved. They will come in and go out, and find pasture. The thief comes only to steal and kill and destroy; I have come that they may have life, and have it to the full.

"I am the good shepherd. The good shepherd lays down his life for the sheep. The hired hand is not the shepherd and does not own the sheep. So when he sees the wolf coming, he abandons the sheep and runs away. Then the wolf attacks the flock and scatters it. The man runs away because he is a hired hand and cares nothing for the sheep.

"I am the good shepherd; I know my sheep and my sheep know me— just as the Father knows me and I know the Father—and I lay down my life for the sheep. I have other sheep that are not of this sheep pen. I must bring them also. They too will listen to my voice, and there shall be one flock and one shepherd. The reason my Father loves me is that I lay down my life—only to take it up again. No one takes it from me, but I lay it down of my own accord.

I have authority to lay it down and authority to take it up again. This command I received from my Father." (Jn. 10:7-18)

How does a shepherd show love for His sheep? He lays down His life for the sheep. If one strays away, he pursues it until it is found.

Then Jesus told them this parable: "Suppose one of you has a hundred sheep and loses one of them. Doesn't he leave the ninety-nine in the open country and go after the lost sheep until he finds it? And when he finds it, he joyfully puts it on his shoulders and goes home. Then he calls his friends and neighbors together and says, 'Rejoice with me; I have found my lost sheep.' (Lk. 15:3-6)

I felt like an insignificant sheep, so I sought human shepherds. If another person saw value in me, perhaps then I would be alright. The truth is, the only One who can give worth is the Lord Jesus, our Shepherd who seeks His lost sheep.

Now I seek out the students who don't seem to belong. They are sad, sorrowful, sullen. Attention-seeking and talkative. Unfocused and unmotivated. Angry. Timid and shy. Gifted but unaware of their gifts. I observe them during activities in class. I try to help them see their value and worth in the eyes of the Creator and to inspire them to see beyond their self-imposed limitations to all they were created to be. I inspire them to see their talents as God-given gifts.

I see myself as a guide and hope-giver to those needing encouragement toward their aspirations and for those who cannot articulate any aspirations at all.

However, I must admit that students I observe are often disruptors. Maybe they do not submit their assignments, or they blurt out irresponsible words in the form of put-downs against themselves or others. Maybe they are constantly reprimanded for talking too much, fidgeting too often, lacking self-control, or not admitting when they are confused or overwhelmed by the lesson content. These are the students who most resemble me during all of my stages of grief as I navigated my fragmented and ever-changing family of origin.

Nor should there be obscenity, foolish talk or coarse joking, which are out of place, but rather thanksgiving. (Eph 5:4)

I stopped going to the teacher's lounge many years ago, which some of my colleagues have criticized. I explained to them that our old school building with an unreliable elevator and too many stairs for my painful knees contribute to my unwillingness to go to the teacher's lounge, given that my classroom is two floors away from the lounge. Although there is some truth to that explanation, the other reason I do not go is that I have been exposed to too many negative depictions of students while sitting in teacher's lounges.

The students who are the most troubled are often on the discipline list or suspended, or they are simply difficult to have in class. These students are often the topic of teacher's lounge conversations, in my experience.

Anger and frustration over how they have derailed our classes and tears of hurt and pure discouragement have filled many teacher's lounges in my twenty-plus years of teaching. Admittedly, I have been a willing participant in the negative descriptions of a student's character at times while being the defender of their character at others.

Conversations with colleagues can degrade into rejoicing at their suspension or expulsion if they were particularly challenging students or if they were a danger to themselves or others. When they were punished, we teachers may have discussed our relief and how they got what they deserved. I realized over time that this type of talk dishonors the student and their family, which is the foolishness the Bible warns against. They, too, are sheep that the Good Shepherd loves.

While I still do not go to the teacher's lounge, I will seek out colleagues who tread carefully concerning the children's behaviors. Some of us, in our imperfect way, strive to honor our students for Jesus' sake since He died for us all. We may discuss more effective ways of teaching these students, and perhaps consult an Academic Intervention Specialist, but understand that dishonoring them in conversation is unkind and ultimately unloving.

> *People were bringing little children to Jesus for him to place his hands on them, but the disciples rebuked them. When Jesus saw this, he was indignant. He said to them, 'Let the little children come to me, and do not hinder them, for the kingdom of God belongs to such as these.*
> *(Mk. 10:13-14)*

My first teaching job was out West. The school system had developed a 'teacher's oath' that I had to recite and confirm by signature that I would abide by. One of the lines was "in loco parentis," Latin for "in the place of a parent." After taking this oath, I focused on being 'parental' – difficult considering I was a 23-year-old who was teaching high school seniors. I actually had one student who was twenty years old. Being so close in age but in a very different season of life, I learned how important it was to value their opinions. I not only had to give their thoughts credence but earn their respect to guide them toward the values I felt it was my duty to uphold. Although I worked in a public-school system and could not display a Bible or speak publicly about my faith (without risking a reprimand or being fired), I prayed regularly to be a positive influence on their souls.

In keeping with this, I attempted to address troubled young people's issues with godly wisdom to help them move beyond negative or self-destructive thoughts and behaviors. I was not as attuned as I am now, but it was in my heart, and much more so after Shaka's death.

CHAPTER 14

WE ARE BELOVED

As indeed he says in Hosea,
"Those who were not my people I will call 'my
people,' and her who was not beloved I will call
'beloved.'" (Romans 9:25) English Standard Version

Children are a wonder. Born completely dependent, we strive to lead them to become autonomous human beings capable of great things. However, their accomplishments along the way can seem small if we are not looking through a shepherd's eyes.

In seventh grade, I moved to a predominantly White state with an African-American population of 4.12%. I lived with my father and his wife (my stepmom and now Grams to my own children) during my middle and high school years. I was the only Black person in all of my classes, which was frightening since I came from D.C., where I saw Black people all the time. My father was from a rural area of another state where he and his siblings worked on his uncle's farm. He loved the beauty of that state and longed to live and work in a similar landscape. When he had the opportunity to move to a mountainous state and continue his career, he did so. I never met his father – my grandfather – but I was told he was a well-educated Black man with a college degree in a time that was nearly impossible. He instilled the need for continued education in his eleven offspring so vigorously that although he died in 1960, which was before I was born, his emphasis lingers for much of my extended family.

In keeping with my grandfather's educational focus, at our family reunions (now a collection of second and third cousins), we celebrate the academic accomplishments of our family members. Unfortunately, this emphasis (although it has its place) has alienated some of our family in largely unintended ways.

Some of my family members are products of involuntary unions between our enslaved ancestors and their White masters (or employees). Thus, the variety of hues in my family is wide. As time has worn on, some of my lighter-skinned family members married White spouses, as did their children. At our reunions, the pigmentation of some cousins shows no sign of their Black heritage, whereas, for others, it is apparent. The diversity of skin-tone and our internal reactions to our enslaved roots has created a low-level of underlying tension during these reunions.

Those of us with darker skin that attracts negative attention and assumptions often want to discuss the common challenges we face. We want to talk about the sorrow and grief that we feel, and discuss how to rise above adversity. We support those who carry the public torches. They are orators sounding the charge to reform and redeem the promises of our forefathers. We strive to honor the sacrifices of those who held the torches in the 1960s that heralded a desperately needed awakening.

However, some of my younger light-skinned cousins do not experience adversity in the same way we darker-skinned cousins have, so our views of life in America differ greatly. It feels awkward to them to have this conversation because our reality is not theirs. We include a book club in our reunion each year. Last year we read *The Hate U Give* by Angie Thomas, and the year before, *The New Jim Crow: Mass Incarceration in the Age of Colorblindness* by Michelle Alexander.

Neither book has real conversation for those who are light-skinned and who "pass for White," as my grandmother used to say. Passing for White always seemed to me to be the best of both worlds. But as I listened to my young cousin at our family reunion, I realized that her reality made her feel like she didn't belong anywhere. She is not White, but she is not dark-skinned and is not recognized as Black, so 'what' is she?

She is a beloved sheep of the Great Shepherd. We must always rejoice in this truth: We are beloved.

> *Jesus answered, "I am the way and the truth and the life. No one comes to the Father except through me." (Jn. 14:6)*

This particular cousin was also frustrated at the number of conversations at our reunions focused on attaining a college degree. "What if college is not for me?" she asked me. What if she wanted to attend a community college? Would she be 'less than' for not attending a four-year university? No! In our reunions, accomplishments are a way to overcome racial adversity and injustices of our past. We must achieve more, work harder, and become more articulate than our White counterparts to be successful. This has been the mantra of my extended family. One of my aunts took the stance that no one is good enough unless they reach a certain pinnacle of academic success. Even my father embodied this idea to some degree.

While I understand its origin and it is ingrained in me to a point, this perspective misses the obvious. Black people have accomplished world-changing status without college degrees, such as Frederick Douglass and others. The truth is, it is Jesus, not other people, who gives us worth. It is His grace, justice, and mercy that will prevail in the end. Our value is not in question in Jesus' eyes. We do not need to prove anything or fear the insults of others. If we seek Him with our lives, we can live victoriously – degree or no degree. Impressing this upon young people is paramount, and we as teachers are in the perfect position to treat our students in ways that bring the truth of God's love to their lives. God's gifts to you require a response, however. Not using your God-given gifts out of fear or anxiety is not the way to go.

So do not fear, for I am with you; do not be dismayed, for I am your God. I will strengthen you and help you; I will uphold you with my righteous right hand. (Isa 41:10)

Who is going to harm you if you are eager to do good? But even if you should suffer for what is right, you are blessed. "Do not fear their threats; do not be frightened." But in your hearts revere Christ as Lord. Always be prepared to give an answer to everyone who asks you to give the reason for the hope that you have. But do this with gentleness and respect, keeping a clear conscience, so that those

who speak maliciously against your good behavior in
Christ may be ashamed of their slander.
(1 Pet. 3:13-16)

So, I rejoice with my young cousin, who is attending community college to be a nurse and help people. As it pertains to the classroom, if a student starts to understand what I am teaching but is not quite there yet, I rejoice with them anyway because perseverance is also an important lesson. If a student blurts out less frequently and shows increased self-control during class, rejoice in that accomplishment because it is a sign of maturing.

In my life, I have experienced put-downs from my family for receiving 'Satisfactory' instead of 'Outstanding' in elementary school; receiving an A- instead of an A+; or anything less than stellar grades. We will be unable to inspire and motivate students to reach their academic, spiritual, and personal potential if meeting our standards how and when we think they should meet them is all that matters. Growth is a gift from the Lord, so acknowledge it when you see it because He is at work in their lives. And pray about your influence over your students.

CHAPTER 15

BE AN ALLY

It always protects, always trusts, always hopes,
always perseveres. (1 Cor. 13:7)

As I mentioned earlier, my husband and I took in young people from time to time. There was one particular girl who had been drawn into an abusive relationship as a result of a fragmented and dysfunctional family of origin. I knew of some specific instances of the dysfunction she had grown up with. One day, while on the phone with a friend, I shared what I knew of her family's drama, using this young lady's name. I spoke freely and without a thought of this family's honor. My husband, who happened to be home at the time, overheard and confronted me about my insensitivity. I paid him no heed at the time, convinced that he was *overly* sensitive. However, the conversation stayed with me over the years, drifting into my consciousness when I found myself tempted to air someone else's painful past.

Finally, it occurred to me that I was self-seeking in those conversations because I wanted to look important. I knew something my friend did not, and I wanted to appear wise because of my involvement in the family's affairs. The truth is, I was not showing love because love always protects. I damaged this young lady in the eyes of others who had never met her but would take her family issues into account and have a soured perspective of her, despite not knowing her. Once information leaves your mouth, the words are no longer yours to control. Someone else will associate their reality, truth, and definition with your words. Some experiences are so very personal and deeply tragic that no one has the right to describe those truths but the one who has experienced them. Another who hears about it, even directly, does not have the right to pontificate or gossip about, express, or interpret the experience themselves.

Love always protects the honor and dignity of a person made in the image of God. If your students have had dreadful lives and you know some deep, dark secrets, or you see how those situations are affecting their behaviors in school, your best option is mentioning what you may know to the school counselors while being wise in your choice of words. The counselors can take it from there with the student and family.

In Shaka's case, I did not mention my concerns regarding his sullenness, withdrawal, and sorrowful nature to the guidance counselors. At the time, I was thinking only about making sure his father knew. What I now know is, many people may need to be involved in supporting a student, but it isn't always up to me to share details. The young person needs to be allowed to choose who they share with. Now, I simply offer to accompany them to a counselor or to sit in with them, making sure to protect their dignity and honor. If they are unwilling to go to the counselor at all, with or without me, and the issue is one of grave importance to their lives or their ability to learn, I will alert the guidance counselor directly. However, how I pass that information on and my purpose for doing so matters to God. The student is His creation, first and foremost.

CHAPTER 16

BE HUMBLE

If I speak in the tongues of men or of angels, but do not have love, I am only a resounding gong or a clanging cymbal. (1 Cor. 13:1)

Students will just hear 'noise' if they do not know they are loved, regardless of your level of professional achievement or your impeccable skills.

We know that "We all possess knowledge." But knowledge puffs up while love builds up. Those who think they know something do not yet know as they ought to know. But whoever loves God is known by God. (1 Cor. 8:1-3)

In this world, many will applaud accomplishments. My extended family's emphasis on academic achievements throughout the years has been suffocating for some. One of my dearest first cousins will not come to the reunions because of her family of origin drama, in part, and also because she is unhappy that she does not have the house with a husband and children, the noteworthy job, and so on…. For some, the American dream. It is a combination of that 'American Dream' and the focus on how we, as Black people, shall overcome. None of that is sinful, but the focus needs to be on the Lord, who is the author and perfecter of our faith. (See Heb 12:2.)

There is nothing wrong with having goals and dreams unless they are prompted by a worldly definition of success (selfish ambition) rather than being based on the mission and purpose of God's calling on your life.

For we are God's handiwork, created in Christ Jesus
to do good works, which God prepared in advance
for us to do. (Eph. 2:10)

If we do not fix our eyes on Jesus and cast our anxiety on Him, then we fix our eyes on the desires of this world, which will fail to satisfy.

Therefore, since we are surrounded by such a great
cloud of witnesses, let us throw off everything that
hinders and the sin that so easily entangles. And
let us run with perseverance the race marked out
for us, fixing our eyes on Jesus, the pioneer and
perfecter of our faith. For the joy set before him
he endured the cross, scorning its shame, and
sat down at the right hand of the throne of God.
Consider him who endured such opposition from
sinners, so that you will not grow weary and lose
heart. (Heb. 12:1-3)

Humble yourselves, therefore, under God's mighty hand, that he may lift you up in due time. Cast your anxiety on him because he cares for you.
(1 Pet. 5:6-7)

Do not love the world or anything in the world. If anyone loves the world, love for the Father is not in them. For everything in the world – the lust of the flesh, the lust of the eyes, and the pride of life – comes not from the Father but from the world. The world and its desires pass away, but whoever does the will of God lives forever. (1 Jn. 2:15-17)

We demonstrate to our students how to cherish the Lord, and in His name, we must also cherish them. The strength of our content knowledge and Bible knowledge, and our ability to communicate this knowledge; our expression of deep faith and prayer life – these do not guarantee that we will exhibit love toward our students. We can possess that entire skillset and not exhibit the love that makes it matter. All that we know will simply sound like 'noise.'

Biblical knowledge, faith, and prayer are all necessary to live out our relationship with Jesus; however, our connection to others – love – is not automatic.

For where you have envy and selfish ambition, there you find disorder and every evil practice. But the wisdom that comes from heaven is first of all pure; then peace-loving, considerate, submissive, full of mercy and good fruit, impartial and sincere. Peacemakers who sow in peace reap a harvest of righteousness. (Jas. 3:16-18)

He is the One to whom we must look for our spiritual and physical needs. Envy and selfish-ambition must be eradicated and surrendered to Him in our lives daily. Ask Him to reveal any unclean way in you.

Search me, God, and know my heart; test me and know my anxious thoughts. See if there is any offensive way in me and lead me in the way everlasting. (Ps. 139:23-24)

I find these particular verses from Psalm 139 to be frighteningly difficult to pray. The harder something is to pray, the more I really need to pray it. I have to act on crucifying any offensive ways that surface during prayer. We must sacrifice and crucify daily in surrender to the One and Only Lord of Hosts.

Our help is in the name of the Lord, the Maker of heaven and earth. (Ps. 124:8)

Our Lord will help our actions align with His when we act on what is true instead of just practicing basic spiritual disciplines. We think that by following rules, God will make us right with Him. But love is a verb, so active changes in how we treat others (our students, colleagues, parents, spouses, and children) are outgrowths of a living and vibrant love, which acts according to God's word. (See 1 Cor. 13:4-8.)

But now you must also rid yourselves of all such things as these: anger, rage, malice, slander, and filthy language from your lips. Do not lie to each other, since you have taken off your old self with

*its practices and have put on the new self, which
is being renewed in knowledge in the image of its
Creator. Here there is no Gentile or Jew, circumcised
or uncircumcised, barbarian, Scythian, slave or
free, but Christ is all, and is in all. Therefore, as
God's chosen people, holy and dearly loved, clothe
yourselves with compassion, kindness, humility,
gentleness and patience. Bear with each other and
forgive one another if any of you has a grievance
against someone. Forgive as the Lord forgave you.*
(Col. 3:8-13)

In this time of racial unrest in America, and, I daresay, in many other places across the globe, we should be mindful of the destructive rhetoric being spoken. It is imperative to lay aside our old selves, which have been influenced by the ways of this world. This influence dates back from antiquity onward: through the Trans-Atlantic Slave Trade, colonialism, apartheid, the mining of blood diamonds, sex trafficking, child endangerment, and the like. We must exchange the impact these experiences have on our psyches for a renewed knowledge of the One who created us. Hearts of compassion, humility, gentleness, and patience will allow us to teach students, befriend colleagues, and live out our faith.

We must allow ourselves to be molded on the Potter's wheel so His purpose and mission can be achieved through us.

*Yet you, Lord, are our Father. We are the clay, you are
the potter; we are all the work of your hand.*
(Isa. 64:8)

But who are you, a human being, to talk back to God? "Shall what is formed say to the one who formed it, 'Why did you make me like this?'" Does not the potter have the right to make out of the same lump of clay some pottery for special purposes and some for common use? (Rom. 9:20-21)

Be alert and of sober mind. Your enemy the devil prowls around like a roaring lion looking for someone to devour. (1 Pet. 5:8)

Surrender in prayer, casting all our anxieties on Him because He cares for us. He will help us be better teachers and guides as we accept his guidance and apply His love to our teaching.

CHAPTER 17

BE A LEARNER

For the Lord gives wisdom; from his mouth come knowledge and understanding. (Prov. 2:6)

The word 'diversity' carries certain connotations. Multi-ethnic, multi-aged, and those with varied life experiences come together to enrich each other by sharing their perspectives. Interestingly, as an inner-city school teacher, I have often had classrooms with students of similar socio-economic backgrounds but not necessarily similar cultures.

Over the years, I have taught students from a wide variety of countries and cultures: Peru, Guatemala, El Salvador, Honduras, Nigeria, Cameroon, Uganda, Ghana, Guyana, the Gambia, Liberia, Vietnam, Latvia, Argentina, Russia, Ukraine, Mexico, Dominican Republic, Ireland, and Haiti, as well as White American and African-American students. I have had to learn how to value other cultures by listening to my students' experiences in their home countries; and to address my own biases, ignorance, and even prejudices. I learned to speak Spanish and a few words in other languages. Students have taught me plenty, as well: how to make tamales, pupusas, arepas, as well as the ingredients in fufu, a Nigerian staple. All of these shared experiences enriched my life and exposed my own children to expanded foods and cultures.

One year, one of my Vietnamese students struggled academically in all of his classes, including mine. He was often absent, and when I tried to talk to him about it, he told me he was having difficulty understanding what was being taught, despite his fluency in English. I began to pay more attention to how he learned and discovered that he more than likely was dealing with a learning difference. Unfortunately, this student didn't want to talk to anyone about that possibility. The student's parents only spoke Vietnamese. Neither of them had a high school education, and they did not comprehend most concepts of the public-school system or the culture of U.S. youth. They struggled to relate to their son. He was impatient and felt stupid, as though he was just not trying hard enough. Eventually, after consulting with other teachers, I realized there was a bias against this student because he appeared Asian, and Asian students are often assumed to be brilliant and ahead of the curve.

The fact that this student may have needed an Individualized Education Program (IEP) had not been explored. When he was a junior in high school, the frustration of his academic challenges led him to drop out of school and join a gang. The final conversation I had with him included him thanking me for trying but telling me that his plan was the best idea. At least he knew I cared for him and that he was of value to someone.

Another student from Liberia was facing placement in foster care because her grandmother, whom she lived with in the United States, had become quite ill, and her parents had been lost to the civil war and unrest in Liberia. All of this affected the success of her learning.

As teachers, we must be sensitive to the different cultures within the U.S. as well as students from other countries. Becoming aware of these cultural differences, customs, and nuances in languages requires humility and compassionate curiosity.

CHAPTER 18

BE PERCEPTIVE

*You have searched me, Lord, and you know me. You
know when I sit and when I rise; you perceive my
thoughts from afar. You discern my going out and
my lying down; you are familiar with all my ways.*
(Ps. 139:1-3)

Over my teaching years, I have encountered many different types of teachers. Early on, some supportive faculty members helped me as a 23-year-old. They were kind and instructed me along the way. However, I have also worked with teachers who were discouraged by some aspects of our chosen career. They complained about how we were treated by students and their parents, administration through government education specialists (those who made decisions regarding our curriculum and a host of other issues), and even the level of cleanliness within our school buildings.

As I have previously mentioned, I now avoid the teacher's lounges, but in the beginning, I did not. I was subjected to the angry words of these disenfranchised staff members who thought some students were lost causes and never going to amount to anything. They stated they did not get paid enough to care for these kids. They would go on to say they were not sacrificing any more of their time and no longer willing to work past three PM. The most repugnant was when a colleague suggested that the students who did not want to learn should be sent to an island with their parents so they would no longer affect the local gene pool.

In 1993, I found myself listening to the 'negative Nancys.' I began to wonder if I could ever teach the ninth graders anything. The Simpsons TV show was popular with the students, who thought it was cute to tell me "don't have a cow, man" (as Bart Simpson would say) when I got upset because they were not paying attention to me. I yelled at my students and cried at home; sometimes I would even cry at school. I was so discouraged that school year that I quit mid-year during Christmas Break. Years later, I learned self-care was the key to my health and happiness while teaching.

At any rate, I broke my year-long contract and set out to find something 'better' and more fulfilling. Something else that would use my talents and perhaps make me more money as well. I was hired to be an educational specialist writer. My boss was a perfectionist and given to fits of anger. Working for her was difficult because she seemed easily angered by me. My health was suffering due to a then undiagnosed illness. My maternal grandfather passed away. My mom was hospitalized for a variety of issues, including knee surgery. Apparently, I had not stumbled upon my nirvana away from teaching, so I took an object-oriented programming course, intending to get out of educational consulting altogether. I applied to several tech companies, given that my degree was in mathematics with a focus on applied math. I landed a position with a government contractor for NASA. It was exciting to work at the Goddard Space Flight Center and to learn about the shuttle program as a software test engineer.

My knowledge of applied math and science grew but at some point, contracts and projects changed. I did not want to work on the new project so I chose a different company to work for instead. This new job provided me an opportunity to not only continue as a software test engineer, but also as a technical writer and a corporate trainer. Although teaching adults was interesting, I began to feel the pull to teach students again.

One lesson I learned was that continual professional development can keep your love for the profession from growing cold. After other jobs in education where I sought to learn more and grow in my craft, I returned to the inner-city classroom with more experience and a renewed sense of purpose.

I worked in one school where it was hard to find teachers who would even smile because the working conditions were so difficult to teach in. A parent told me that she did not understand why I was calling about her child's behavior because I was the one present so I was supposed to deal with it. I also had students who, in large part, came to school to be with friends but not to learn. Their elementary years had been fraught with teacher substitutes and absenteeism and the lack of consistency left them just happy to see their friends. Their focus was not on future careers or life goals, only surviving and socializing. As a result, I started soul-searching again about what I wanted to do with education because I was miserable in my new situation.

One day, one of my students arrived in my classroom late. She was wearing sunglasses on that cloudy day and would not remove them when asked. In addition, she was rude to me and combative about it so I let the situation go. After her third day wearing them, she removed them so that I could see why she was wearing them. A big black, blue, and yellow bruise completely covered one eye, extending to her forehead and cheek. I asked if there had been a fight with another student, given that she was fairly boastful and mouthy. I was stunned to learn that her parent had beat her by punching her repeatedly after receiving a phone call that she had a D in one of my classes. I was mortified to hear that this beating was a direct result of my own phone call to the parent. After Child Protective Services was called and I completed a report, I learned that CPS had been sent to that particular home at least five times since this student started high school, and she was only a junior.

In another class, one of my students was a football player and a good actor, but he kept falling asleep in class. Initially, I thought this student did not want to learn, was bored, or was incapable of performing well in my course. I was so frustrated that I called his parent to complain. After receiving multiple reassurances by phone that he would get better, his mom finally informed me that the student was on a medication that caused his drowsiness. She and the pediatrician then addressed his needs with alternative prescriptions. With the medical situation resolved, the student's giftedness in mathematics surfaced. After a few months, I encouraged him to pursue engineering as a high school academy choice in our school. We still keep in touch.

Relying on the Lord in prayer to help perceive the needs of your students is imperative. I have learned that students' behaviors can be due to many factors at work in their lives outside of your control as a teacher. Always hope that the Lord will lead your students to Himself and pray for them continually. Step outside of the situation and follow the Lord's example of love and "keep no record of wrongs." Love always hopes.

CHAPTER 19

BE PERSEVERANT

Watch your life and doctrine closely. Persevere in them, because if you do, you will save both yourself and your hearers. (1 Tim. 4:16)

Perseverance has to be part of a teacher's toolkit. Without it, discouragement shows up and moves in until your career ends.

For me, persevering in education has been a focal point because I have been 'called' to educate time and time again, despite discouragement. How and why do I stay in a profession that has so many drawbacks at face value? Compensation, resources, respect, work-life balance, and temperaments of students, colleagues, and parents can all be considered negatives in this profession from time to time. Yet, I have fought, with myself largely, to stay in the teaching career because the profession is, for me, a ministry to the hearts of young people.

My passion is for students to exercise their God-given gifts of heart and mind to His glory. Focusing on them and providing light on their journey through high school is what I do for Him and them.

> *Therefore, since we have been justified through faith, we have peace with God through our Lord Jesus Christ, through whom we have gained access by faith into this grace in which we now stand. And we boast in the hope of the glory of God. Not only so, but we also glory in our sufferings, because we know that suffering produces perseverance; perseverance, character; and character, hope. And hope does not put us to shame, because God's love has been poured out into our hearts through the Holy Spirit, who has been given to us. You see, at just the right time, when we were still powerless, Christ died for the ungodly. (Rom. 5:1-6)*

Our youth are fragile and powerless in many ways, just as we are before the Lord. He died for us while we were ungodly and powerless. As teachers, we are to act 'in loco parentis' who give their lives for their children when needed and sacrifice to help them be successful. Sometimes, as in the examples above, parents are not as sacrificial as the child may need or may even be abusive, but there is still God's love.

> *But Zion said, The Lord has forsaken me, the Lord has forgotten me. Can a mother forget the baby at her breast and have no compassion on the child she has borne? Though she may forget, I will not forget you! See, I have engraved you on the palms of my hands; your walls are ever before me. (Isa. 49:14-16)*

God has not forgotten the student. He has placed us here to stand in the gap for them. As Christian teachers, we protect, care about, educate, and pray for the Lord's guidance for our students so they may see His love, no matter where their faith may be. Persevere in showing God's love for your students so they can see that it never fails. They will need your strength, insight, and all of the fruits of the Holy Spirit to not only strive for God's best for their lives but to thrive while pursuing Him.

But the fruit of the Spirit is love, joy, peace,
forbearance, kindness, goodness, faithfulness,
(Gal. 5:22)

Abiding in Christ as the vine while we are the branches will produce fruit in our lives. The Fruit of the Spirit bears, first of all, love – not any love, but God's love, which can then be poured out on others. Goodness, faithfulness, gentleness, and self-control should be evident in our classrooms in increasing measure, all the days of our teaching profession and beyond.

For this very reason, make every effort to add to your faith goodness; and to goodness, knowledge; and to knowledge, self-control; and to self-control, perseverance; and to perseverance, godliness; and to godliness, mutual affection; and to mutual affection, love. For if you possess these qualities in increasing measure, they will keep you from being ineffective and unproductive in your knowledge of our Lord Jesus Christ. (2 Pet. 1:5-8)

Consider it pure joy, my brothers and sisters,
whenever you face trials of many kinds, because
you know that the testing of your faith produces

perseverance. Let perseverance finish its work so that you may be mature and complete, not lacking anything. (Jas. 1:2-4)

Maturity and completeness, not lacking anything, comes from perseverance that passes the testing of our faith. Teaching challenging students does test our faith. Still, keep the faith; strive for goodness, knowledge, and self-control; persevere in kind and patient love, learning to keep no record of wrongs; don't be rude, boastful, dismissive, or disingenuous. Submitting to God, practicing spiritual discipline, seeking godly counsel, and taking care of all facets of our own health provides the foundation for guiding our students.

The Lord bless you and keep you; the Lord make his face shine on you and be gracious to you; the Lord turn his face toward you and give you peace. (Num. 6:24-26)

- ❖ We have an ASTRONOMICAL **INFLUENCE**
- ❖ We must ACTIVELY **INSPIRE**
- ❖ We must strive to have an AWESOME **IMPACT**
- ❖ We must ACCESS **INNOVATION**

1. Our ultimate calling is to influence others for Christ.
2. Inspire your students to work harder than they ever thought they could.
3. Innovate your lessons for effective content delivery with your students' future educational needs in mind.
4. Impact your students for the Lord.

By doing these four "I"s for your students, they will be equipped to not only strive but thrive in their knowledge of your content as well as in their practice and receipt of the Lord Jesus Christ's love for them and their love for others.

CHAPTER 20

INSPIRE

*The student is not above the teacher, but everyone
who is fully trained will be like their teacher. Why do
you look at the speck of sawdust in your brother's
eye and pay no attention to the plank in your own
eye? How can you say to your brother, 'Brother,
let me take the speck out of your eye,' when you
yourself fail to see the plank in your own eye? You
hypocrite, first take the plank out of your eye, and
then you will see clearly to remove the speck from
your brother's eye. (Lk. 6:40-42)*

When I was 27, I taught in a high school where I met
a 23-year-old teacher – a newbie. Since she was
younger than me, I thought I would show her the ropes, so
to speak. I spent a lot of time trying to help her acclimate to
her classroom. Your first year of teaching is nerve-wracking,
especially if you have a soft-spoken personality and teach
high school in the inner-city/urban public-school system.

She became so frustrated by the lack of attentiveness from her students who would ignore her, play with their Gameboys, or listen to music while she was teaching, that she decided to divide the room in half. On one side were those who wanted to learn. On the other were those who, in her opinion, did not. She taught to one side of the room. I attempted to get her to see that if those students who were being difficult had been her brothers or sisters, nieces or nephews, she would not be happy with a teacher who did this to them. She was stuck because she really wanted to teach Math, but she was not interested in connecting on a heart level with the students. Administration can help us in these situations; however, those are ideas for another book.

My first full-time job in a high school classroom was in 1989. I taught in a traditional setting from 1989 – 1994. In 1994, I left the classroom to pursue other interests, and between 1994 and 2011, my husband and I adopted two children, fostered two others, and were surrogate parents/ mentors to eight more. During those years, I stayed home with my children while working odd jobs. We owned a janitorial business for a while until my health became an issue. After we stopped cleaning offices, I began working part-time for Huntington Learning Center as a head teacher and then as an academic instructor at the Junior Tennis Champions Center. For those sixteen years, although I was still teaching and working in education, it was not in a traditional classroom environment.

The D.C. area school where I taught back in 1991 had a population of around 2,000 students, with over 90% being African-American. One of my students was shot in a drive-by. My entire senior math class felt confident that their high school education was unnecessary because of the probability that they wouldn't live to see twenty-one.

Their fatalism was well earned considering that in 1991, according to The Journal of Trauma and Acute Care, Article Violence in America: A Public Health Crisis -- The Role of Firearms; The Violence Prevention Task Force of the Eastern Association for the Surgery of Trauma:

> *The most common cause of death in 15- to 24-year-old black American males is firearm homicide. Their annual death rate from this cause has increased 61% between 1979 and 1989, and it has been rising more rapidly than for any other cause.*

Violence in America: A Public Health Crisis--The Role of Firearms: Journal of Trauma and Acute Care Surgery (lww.com)

By the time these young people were high school seniors, they had witnessed hatred, violence, and death. They had access to guns and truly expected their lives to be cut short.

In 1993, I was working in another school further into Maryland. One of my most dedicated students and her twin were in my ninth-grade Algebra 1 course. On a Saturday, they had gone to a birthday party near their grandmother's house and were heading back there when the shooting started. A stray bullet struck this student during a gunfire exchange between other people. Her twin caught her in his arms, and she died there on the sidewalk. I found out on Monday morning. My heart was broken again, and terror and fear gripped my young students as their hopes for their lives were dashed to the ground. *"What is in store for us?"* they worried. That same year we ended up on lockdown when adults from rival gangs made it into our school building with guns. Regarding the student we all lost, I still reach out to her mother sometimes to share the hurt of missing that bright and loving young lady.

Many things in society changed dramatically in those sixteen years. When I returned to the traditional classroom in 2011, I was shocked at the drastic difference in the students' relationships with their teachers. I found that my students had developed profound neediness for affirmation, recognition, and hand-holding, unable to motivate themselves to pursue learning for their own sake. They experienced a different type of resignation-like fatalism that their lives were meaningless, even if they lived into adulthood.

Their academic apathy and lethargy were discouraging until I realized that I could reach these students by helping them find their God-given intellectual capabilities. Many of my students were accustomed to thinking lowly of themselves, discounting their intellect and purpose in life. Regardless of their circumstances, they demonstrated a collective malaise. What they needed was a dose of genuine concern. I wanted them to understand their lives were too precious to waste.

I had a near-death scare: a pesky tumor, an invasive surgery, and a long recovery, during which I spent a lot of time considering this gift of life. Before my final diagnosis and deciding on a treatment plan, I was getting ready to die and putting my affairs in order. Now, I can see that His mercies are new every morning. Despite my continuing health challenges, I choose to be upbeat and thankful for the lives I have the daily opportunity to touch.

*Because of the Lord's great love we are not
consumed, for his compassions never fail. They are
new every morning; great is your faithfulness.*
(Lam. 3:22-23)

When I was in graduate school, I completed a course entitled "Teaching as Performing." The goal of this course was to help each teacher take command of a classroom and understand how the environment (including our own attire and how we expect to be addressed) impacted the students' willingness to learn. I took these lessons to heart then as I could see the effect for myself as they tested their theories on us as their students. I take those lessons to heart now as I am pragmatically aware of how the learning environment affects my own students. When a student attends a school with newer classrooms, nice bathrooms, and a clean cafeteria that offers delicious options at reasonable prices, they tend to feel valued. However, for students attending school in a worn-down building, devoid of the comforts of air conditioning or clean bathrooms, and staffed by teachers who don't display warmth toward them, the environment often fosters challenging behaviors.

I have taught in schools built in the 1950s and minimally maintained, and I have worked in more modern school buildings. Students treat their spaces differently based on perceived value and importance. With few exceptions, conversations with students over the years have revealed the inferiority they feel when their classrooms are not inviting or lack equipment or when teachers operate as if their students are nuisances.

Virtually or physically adorning your classroom with scripture or inspiring quotes can call the student to think more deeply, perhaps even causing them to seek the Lord. I keep my classroom covered with inspirational posters with themes such as perseverance, teamwork, hard work, and other traits our students ourselves should aim to manifest. I pray over their seats or their names to set the necessary environment, especially within myself, to help them learn and feel loved. Our students need to know we are interested in them as people and not just how they do with what we assign them. One of my wall posters is below:

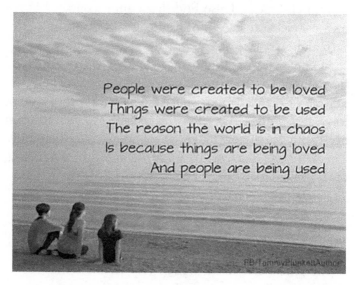

People were created to be loved
Things were created to be used
The reason the world is in chaos
Is because things are being loved
And people are being used

I try to choose wise sayings with people who look like them to encourage them to ponder substantive ideas. One day as we took our laptops for class from the cart sitting below the above sign, a ninth-grader said, "Wow, Ms. Ming. That is profound and so true!" We were able to speak more about what was happening in her life because she read the poster. Students can and will think about what surrounds them in class, even in a virtual setting, as we are using now.

Using a "Scripture of the Day" (or week) can remind students to seek strength from God through His Word, especially as the pandemic rages on, protests abound, and deaths continue to rise. We, as teachers, stand in the gap. I have included a few posters for you to use, if you choose. There are more on the following website: https://www.charactercounts.org/, along with other resources to help you instill, or at least reference, the importance of character in your classroom. I also find that I am encouraged in my own character as I seek to inspire, equip, and minister to each and every one of my students.

I pray that this glimpse into my life has provided 'food for thought' as you support your own students. Their lives outside of the classroom affect them in ways they cannot leave at the door. Ask God for a sharp eye and an open heart, and watch how He helps you minister to their souls. The Lord can use you to usher them to the everlasting waters where they can drink and be satisfied.

The Conclusion of the Matter:

Ecclesiastes 12:13: Now all has been heard; here is the conclusion of the matter: Fear God and keep his commandments, for this is the duty of all mankind.

Micah 6:8: He has shown you, O mortal, what is good. And what does the LORD require of you? To act justly and to love mercy and to walk humbly with your God.

I think the purpose of life is to be useful, to be responsible, to be honorable, to be compassionate. It is, after all, to matter: to count, to stand for something, to have made some difference that you lived at all.
–Leo C. Rosten

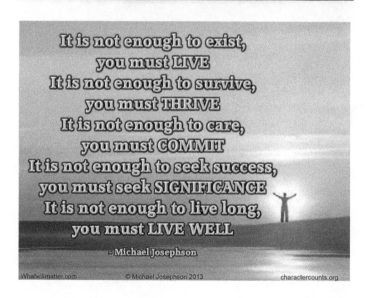

It is not enough to exist,
you must LIVE
It is not enough to survive,
you must THRIVE
It is not enough to care,
you must COMMIT
It is not enough to seek success,
you must seek SIGNIFICANCE
It is not enough to live long,
you must LIVE WELL

- Michael Josephson

Whatwillmatter.com   © Michael Josephson 2013   charactercounts.org

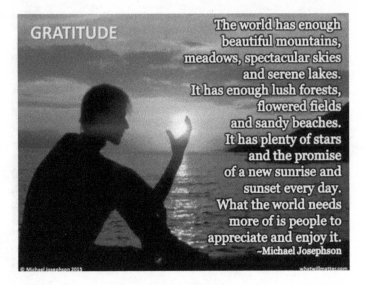

GRATITUDE

The world has enough
beautiful mountains,
meadows, spectacular skies
and serene lakes.
It has enough lush forests,
flowered fields
and sandy beaches.
It has plenty of stars
and the promise
of a new sunrise and
sunset every day.
What the world needs
more of is people to
appreciate and enjoy it.
~Michael Josephson

© Michael Josephson 2015

whatwillmatter.com

APPENDIX A

Shaka Franklin Foundation Website

<u>SFF's Story</u>
The Shaka Franklin Foundation for Youth began when 16-year-old Shaka Franklin took his own life. This tragic incident sparked a light in his father, Les Franklin, who believed that suicide among youths was growing at increasingly alarming rates.

Since its inception in 1990, the non-profit has fought tirelessly to address suicide among youths in Colorado and to those across the nation.

The organization helps the youth by providing appropriate education, support, and awareness to those in need.

www.shaka.org

Suicide Prevention Resources

National Suicide Prevention Lifeline

We can all help prevent suicide. The Lifeline provides 24/7, free and confidential support for people in distress; prevention and crisis resources for you or your loved ones; and best practices for professionals.

1-800-273-8255
https://suicidepreventionlifeline.org/

APPENDIX B

Racial Healing

Traces of the Trade Documentary

Inheriting the Trade Book written by Thomas Norman DeWolf

The Uncomfortable Truth Documentary by Loki Mulholland

The Little Book of Racial Healing by Thomas Norman DeWolf

Proud Recipient of 2021-22 PLTW
Outstanding Teacher of the Year Award